Unveiling the Diva Mystique

Michelle McKinney Hammond

D0067576

HARVEST HOUSE PUBLISHERS

EUGENE, OREGON

Published in association with the literary agency of Alive Communications, Inc., 7680 Goddard Street, Ste #200, Colorado Springs, CO 80920.

THE DIVA PRINCIPLE is a series trademark of Michelle McKinney Hammond. Harvest House Publishers, Inc., is the exclusive licensee of the trademark THE DIVA PRINCIPLE.

Cover photo by Ernest Collins; makeup: Joseph Hampton

Cover by Koechel Peterson & Associates, Inc., Minneapolis, Minnesota

UNVEILING THE DIVA MYSTIQUE
Copyright © 2005 by Michelle McKinney Hammond
Published by Harvest House Publishers
Eugene, Oregon 97402
www.harvesthousepublishers.com

Library of Congress Cataloging-in-Publication Data
McKinney Hammond, Michelle, 1957-
    Unveiling the diva mystique / Michelle McKinney Hammond.
        p. cm.
    ISBN-13: 978-0-7369-1548-9 (pbk.)
    ISBN-10: 0-7369-1548-6 (pbk.)
    1. Christian women—Religious life.   2. Attitude (Psychology)—Religious aspects—
Christianity.   3. Women in the Bible—Biography.   4. Success—Religious aspects—
Christianity.   5. Conduct of life.   I. Title.
    BV4527.M425 2005
    248.8'43—dc22   2005001900

Printed in the United States of America

05   06   07   08   09   10   11   12   /   VP-MS   /   10   9   8   7   6   5   4   3   2   1

To those who have never given themselves
permission to feel beautiful...

To those who have no idea how powerful
and rich they really are...

Choose today to celebrate the discovery
of all that God has placed within you.

Acknowledgments

To the women in my family who are the most amazing blend of little girls and ancient sages. Who display the most incredible range of emotions from naïve wonderment to razor-sharp discernment. I want to be like you all when I grow up.

To my Harvest House family, you have nurtured this diva into being.

To all those who lift up my arms with your prayers, encouragement, and service. There would be no me without you. Take a deep bow; I honor you.

Contents

The Real Deal

All right ladies, here we go. It's time to bump it up a notch—to stretch, reach, and transcend to the next level of truly victorious living. It's not enough to just look the part, my sisters, we've got to dig deep and settle some foundational issues. Why? Because life happens. Every day is not a walk through the tulips. Situations press against us. Circumstances erupt around us. People go off on us. Events rock us. Words hurt us. What is a diva to do in a less-than-pleasant scenario? Maintain her diva-tude, of course. But that can't happen unless some internal matters have been dealt with and settled. What is on the inside will come out if squeezed hard enough. And rest assured, people will put you to the test, find your last nerve, and hop all over it. If you don't watch out, you can completely lose it, despite the fact that you are dressed to impress. What we harbor internally can truly ruin the external if we don't have a grip on our thoughts and responses to the changes people can put us through.

However, we must also be honest with ourselves: No one makes us do anything—people just push our buttons. We manifest our true selves in those instances and regret our explosions later. It is perfectly normal to react first and think later. But we're about to flip the script, put all that to rest, and work on our inner selves—the beneath-the-surface, secret, true life of a diva. The place where the foundation of diva-hood is firmly entrenched in our inner woman, in our spirit. From there, it merely works its way outward and complements our outer beauty. Yes, my sister, true beauty, as well as diva-hood, comes from within. If you read my first installment of this premise, *The Diva Principle*™ (Harvest House, 2004), you may recall the true definition of diva means divine. Yes, we've been created to reflect the divine nature of God Himself in all we say and do. I know that won't be hard for you because if you picked up this book, you are already committed to being the best you can possibly be. Therefore, the major work is already done—making the decision to grow beyond where you presently stand. Together we will take a look at some amazing women who have gone before us, yet dealt with some of the same issues and struggles we face today. And they emerged in true diva fashion—with the type of grace and courage that left a positive, life-changing impression on those around them. If experience is a fabulous teacher, truly there is something to be said for those who learned the lessons and are willing to pass them on. Let's learn by example and hopefully be spared the pain of learning from negative experiences. I realize some things can only be taught through experience, but for those cases where examples will suffice, I suggest you take advantage and keep on stepping. It's called wisdom, ladies.

As we take this journey together, I will ask you to be brutally honest with yourself. Which areas do you need to work on? Where do your true struggles lie? And what stops you from having victory over these various areas? Though you may not always like your answers, keep in mind that what you don't acknowledge you cannot fix.

Life is not about the destination; it is all about the journey and the transformation that occurs along the way. As our minds are renewed, our lives are transformed as a result. What we think affects what we do. What we do attracts a response or reaction that either gets us close enough to grasp what we want or drives us further away from it. The choice is more within our control than we realize. Right choices have everything to do with a right outcome. That power lies in your hands and your hands alone. You may not be able to control other people, but you *can* control yourself. Therefore, let's go beneath the surface and deal with the core of who we are as women. Keep the good, and get rid of the bad. Down with stinkin' thinkin' and up with right attitudes and sound wisdom. We are on a mission to capture the true essence of divine womanhood—defined and manifested by sound character, sterling integrity, and God's amazing grace.

Don't be too hard on yourself and get hung up on past mistakes or perceived failures. As your understanding becomes more enlightened, remember all the good, bad, and ugly have culminated to make you the woman you are today. It all works out for the good if you've chosen to learn your lessons along the way. Did I say make sure you grab a journal for the journey? You're gonna need it. Take notes, talk to yourself, do some self-examination, and make some concrete decisions about where you go from here. We're going for a long-term positive effect for our lives. Chronicle your new commitments on paper so you can stick to them. Remember, we are in this thing together. I'm feeling this, are you? Now...take a deep breath, shoulders back. We can do this. Get ready to take it to the next level. I'll meet you there...

Make a Name for Yourself

Faces without names
    remaining engrafted in history
        though seemingly invisible in present day.
    These are those
        who, driven by a call
            greater than their nature,
                did what they had to do in the moment,
        sending ripples through time
            that remained long after they were gone.
    These are the nameless...
yet someone took note
  of a word,
an action,
an inflection,
    a question that brought conviction
        without accusation,
            yet did its silent work,
                attaching its merit to
                    no one in particular.
These are those who perpetuate change...
    never thinking of taking the credit,
        simply of finishing the task.
These are those who rearrange nations...
    the fabric of society,
        the hearts of men.
These are those who leave their mark...
    without attaching their signature,
for their works speak volumes
    of who they are,
        leaving no need for introduction....
These are the nameless
  who are
    not so nameless after all.

WHAT'S IN A NAME?

*T*here's a lot to be said for a name. The mere mention of a name incites a positive or negative reaction depending on what that name is associated with. Fear, disgust, pride, deep affection, admiration, awe, excitement....Truly the association of our names to a good family, cause, or accomplishment validates us and gives us a great sense of self. Of course, the opposite is deep shame, low self-esteem, anger, and perhaps even hopelessness as you consider rising above your situation and living the life of your dreams.

Obviously God thinks names are important because He took the time to deliberately name many of those we read about in the Bible. A name actually serves as the statement of your profession, a prophecy on who or what you would become. Literally, in the true sense, you are your name. Think about it, everywhere you turn people speak your name. Scripture clearly states in James that the power of life and death is in the tongue. What does that mean when it comes to your name? Every time someone utters your name, they utter a confession about who you are. Because words have spiritual power, the moment those words hit the atmosphere they set in motion spiritual dynamics that cause you to line up with what has been spoken over you. My name "Michelle" means, "who is like God, one who stands behind and practices absolute truth." Now that's a lot to live up to, but I am driven to fulfill exactly that purpose. Perhaps this is why God deliberately changed a few folks' names as He transformed their character. They could no longer be called something that would yank them back to their old nature. They were called to "represent" their new nature. That name revealed who they truly were to those around them in one word, giving those they encountered a clue about the character of the person who stood before them.

As we strive for recognition and prestige in the world today, names are still important. Who we are or who we know can gain us entré or get us excluded from places, positions, or events. Small wonder we clamor to be known. We get hung up on who gets the credit for great accomplishments, how we are treated, the perks we receive for accomplishing the daunting task of "making a name for ourselves." The search for significance consumes a lot of folks, while many an unspoken hero goes quietly about the task of being an invisible blessing, unappreciated by most on earth. However, note is being taken big time in the heavens where credits last along with eternal reward.

What a relief to know, that although you may feel as if your efforts have not received the kudos they should, your contributions will have far-reaching implications unbeknownst to you. As we take a look at some women who remain nameless, glean from them and their stories. See the big picture. Get a handle on what is truly important. Know that your "name" is being written where it will matter most. You see, true divas don't seek earthly recognition. Theirs is a higher call—to affect nations and kingdoms to come by simply doing what the core of their soul, led by the Spirit of God, directs them to do. They seek no greater glory than accomplishing the task at hand. Pride is not a part of the diva nature because she draws all power from a Source higher and greater than herself. In that, she rests and does what she does best—fulfill her destiny by living up to her name whether the rest of the world knows it or not.

The Diva Influence

*T*rue love and fulfillment. These are the two most sought-after commodities in all the world. If everyone wants them, why aren't they more available? Perhaps we are looking in the wrong places. Or, perhaps we attach an unachievable definition to our dreams that guarantees their escape from us. But for a true diva, the search for these precious commodities can never be in vain because she becomes the originator of what she seeks. (Read John 4:1-42.)

Behind the Veil

Squinting into the noonday sun, she prepared herself—mind and body—for the trek to the well. The path was clear. No one would be there now. The blazing orb in the sky at its fullest had resigned the city to a time out until the heat retreated and allowed those beneath its supervision to breathe and move again. This was the time she preferred to take the winding path in solitude, oblivious to the heat that saturated her clothes, making them heavier than they were, while taking the extra effort to draw wind through her nostrils. This was far easier to endure than the stares of disapproval that met her anytime she encountered the citizens of the city.

How ironic that the arms of one good man could leave her lonelier than ever. Perhaps it wasn't fair to phrase it that way....After all, she had had five husbands. She knew many of the women in town were angry with her because they hadn't had one, and she had exhausted their options in their opinion. Those who were married avoided her, tugging their husbands behind them should she get any ideas to add to the list of suitors who seemed to line up awaiting their turn. Even the maids they sent to the well behaved as if they must protect the interests of their mistresses by refusing to offer her any pleasantries. All she wanted was love and peace. Was that too much to ask? What was a woman to do? She, who could not control the ways of men, did not allow death or abandonment to cause her to remain loveless, she merely moved on to the next available arms. And though she was not alone, she found herself very lonely. After all, a man can only fill so much space in a woman's heart and bed before she begins to long for other avenues of fellowship to complete her.

A wry smile curled the corner of her lips as she contemplated her peers' condemnation. Oh well, why do anything halfway? It was simply not her style. If she must be disliked, why not go all the way? Be despised for being a Samaritan woman and a woman with a questionable past. She was beyond feeling anymore. She merely erected her own personal boundaries to deflect the arrows others sought to throw. Some might have thought her haughty. She called it doing what she had to do to protect herself. After all, at the end of the day, man or no man, she was all she had.

Lost in her thoughts, she heard Him before she saw Him. "Give me a drink," He said. The soft-spoken request jolted her from the depths of her thoughts and transported her into a pair of eyes that looked as if they held a thousand secrets. Eyes that for once did not look through her. Though they looked at her, they did not lust for her. Instead, they seemed to penetrate even deeper, to a place where her very soul was unmasked in one glance. And then she noticed His clothes. The clothes of a Jewish rabbi. Why was a Jewish rabbi addressing her? Before she could think, the words escaped her, "How is it that You being a Jew would ask for a drink from a Samaritan woman?" Didn't He know that Jews have no dealings with Samaritans? That rabbis did not converse with women openly in public, especially alone? She was used to conversing with men. That wasn't a problem, but this unusual man with remarkable eyes was boldly breaking all the rules.

Her question did not seem to move Him one way or the other. He continued His intriguing conversation by hinting He was not just any man and what He had to offer her would be better anyway. Believe me, she had received promises of satisfaction from men before, but let's face it, the reality was never as fulfilling as what was foretold. But something was different about Him. He did not leer, or flirt, or seem to surreptitiously try to seduce her. No, He rather confidently told her of water that could do more than eliminate her thirst. It could actually take away her craving for more.

Did He really know what He was saying? she wondered. She longed for so much more—something that could put the desire she harbored so deeply to rest. What did she have to lose? She wanted the water He spoke of. She had grown weary of the journey back and forth each time, seeking to fill and refresh what seemed to be a bottomless chasm in her soul, as well as her body, and she told Him so. He responded to her request, "Go call your husband and come here."

Ah, it was as if a fine surgeon's blade had found its way between her ribs, piercing her heart and the center of her soul. "I have no husband," she quietly replied. All of the self-conserving bravado was gone, and the real woman stood before Him, unpretentious and yet strangely unafraid of His response. His words were accurate but nonjudgmental. "You've answered well, you have no husband, for you have had five husbands and the one you now have is not your husband, so you have spoken truly." It was almost as if He celebrated her for her honesty even though the truth was not the best of circumstances to confess. A prophet who did not condemn and chasten her to turn from her wicked ways? Perhaps she could finally get the answers that burdened her heart. It wasn't that she didn't want to properly worship God, she simply didn't know how. And here He was speaking of eternal rivers and worshipping God in spirit and in truth, of not being religious, but living for God from the heart.

Revealing Himself to be the Messiah, He was the one she had been waiting for to make sense of all her emptiness and shame, and to deliver her from her inward pain and bondage. As the veil fell away from her eyes, she felt her burdens and questions go with it. Her thirst was gone, replaced with a passion to share what she knew with others. Laying aside the water vessel, she faced the city she had run from. Openly addressing the men she had only spoken to in secret before, she beseeched them to come and see this Man who had told her everything she had ever done!

Casting off all decorum, "the men" followed her and learned of Jesus for themselves, and came to believe. This one woman found herself not so alone after all because she, like every other true diva, came to know the true Source of all she desired.

SHE COULD HAVE: Remained so jaded and unresponsive she would have missed the opportunity for her heart to be unlocked, reawakened, and filled to overflowing. She could have been prideful and unwilling to be honest with herself and with the only One who had the real answer for her pain. She could have remained tucked away in the prison of her own denial, never allowing her heart to see the light of day.

WHAT SEPARATES THE DIVAS FROM THE GIRLS: Honesty and a transparent spirit that is open to change. Divas do not pretend to know more than they know. They choose to recognize that Jesus has the answers they have been seeking. They risk becoming vulnerable to obtain the change they want for their lives.

LIFE LESSON: The love, peace, and fulfillment we seek cannot be found in anything made or contained within the confines of human frailty. There is only One who satisfies and refreshes from a place of endless supply. For that which we crave is supernaturally divine and must be poured from the hand of God Himself.

Man shall not live by bread alone, but by every word that proceeds from the mouth of God (Matthew 4:4).

Divas Keep It Real

Men! Can't live with 'em. Can't kill 'em. Let's face it, even while they are sleeping, unaware of the swirling emotions around them, they are able to keep even a major diva spinning off her center. We can bring home the bacon, fry it up in a pan, but where's our man who fulfills our every dream of the ultimate type of fulfillment? Many a modern-day diva has triumphed in the area of building her personal empire complete with achievements, accolades, and material possessions, but finds that the one terrain still unconquered and, in some cases, undiscovered is the area of love and true fulfillment. Though they have drunk from the cup of success, they find themselves still thirsty.

Cycles of repeat failed relationships only deepen the inner well most women harbor, leaving it more parched than before with each withdrawal allowed by one seen as a potential source of refreshment. And so they seek to fill the well within with more things, experiences, and achievements only to find satisfaction fleeting at best. Those who are married often blame the faults of their husband, from the minute to major, for their discontent. Singles sometimes blame the absence of a man altogether for their feelings of emptiness and low self-worth. In the end, what can a diva do to get a breakthrough? If the question we all struggle with is, What do we have to do in order to be enough to get the love we want? then truly the answer is simpler than we think. Perhaps the question needs to change. Perhaps it is not the lovers who have disappointed us, but our own expectations. If we go seeking results from a medicine whose ingredients were never designed to fulfill, the onus

is not on the prescription, but on the one seeking relief.
Perhaps it's time to learn from our diva at the well how to
be a satisfied lover once and for all.

1. Know what you want.

Notice I didn't say *who?* That would be putting
the cart before the horse. This might call for
several lists in your journal. You might need to
do one for your life and then do the one for
love. Remember, you can always get a package,
but it might not necessarily contain what you
are looking for. Taking note of what you want
and why you want it might be the place to start.
Sometimes the whys reveal unrealistic expectations you will have to revisit and change in
order to get what you want from this exercise.

Perhaps the next thing to ask yourself would be, Why do
you want what you want? What need will this thing or
person fill within you? Are you setting yourself up to be
unhappy later? For instance, if your ability to feel loved is
based on one person and that person disappears, would
you feel any less loved? Then perhaps he should not be the
basis for something so crucial to your state of well-being.

Miss Diva at the Well knew what she wanted. She made
a beeline for the source of water and refreshing she craved.
However, after she arrived, Someone introduced her to the
idea that something better existed. Not something different
from what she wanted, just something of a better quality.
Because she understood why she wanted the water, she was
definitely open to the idea of having her needs met in a way

that was sustainable. And isn't that it? We all want sustainable joy, peace, love, and fulfillment! Ah...but what would it take to have that? Better yet, what could be keeping us from laying hold of it? This is where some deep soul-searching must be done.

2. Be brutally honest and transparent.

Sometimes the truth hurts, but it will also set you free. No room for staying in denial. Our girlfriend at the well had to get real with herself and with Jesus in order to get her breakthrough. There was no room for pride, stylin', or profilin'. She wanted something He had. No, she *needed* it. That is being even more honest. In order to admit you need something, you really have to make yourself vulnerable. Now, now, I realize most of us are not comfortable with the "v" word, but no one can come in if you don't open the door. Any time we open up, something on the inside will be exposed. What are you hiding? The fact you are a real woman in need of love? This is not a crime or a disgrace. We were made to love and be loved. It is actually a natural instinct. No wonder we can't get away from the longing!

This next round of honesty may be more difficult than the first. What is keeping you from getting what you need? Someone once said until the pain of staying the same is greater than the pain of change, you won't change. What needs to change in your world? Your thoughts? habits?

people who are not conducive to you reaching your goal? All of these need to be examined to make way for a better life—not the life you were ready to settle for. You see, our sister at the well was willing to settle for water from Jacob's well until she found out there was some better water to be had. But she had to do something to get it. She had to bring everything she had to the party and confess what she didn't have. Ouch! She knew deep down she had some lifestyle issues that needed to be corrected. She had to be honest in order to qualify for complete peace and fulfillment. It was not enough to simply know what she wanted, she also had to know who she was, where she was, and how she had been contributing to her own problem.

It is not clear from the story if she had been married five times or had five affairs. It is not clear if she was in an adulterous relationship when she met Jesus at the well, or if she was simply living with the man she was with. But we do know this much from that amount of information, girlfriend was locked in a cycle. Or should I say trapped between a revolving door that was draining her instead of filling her. It took Jesus making her say out loud what she inwardly knew—she was not in the right position to receive what she really wanted. Only by her own heartfelt admission to this could she then be empowered to make a change in her life.

3. Be open.

Sometimes we decide in life only one way works for us. We become religious about our personal rituals. Methodical in the way things must be done in our lives in order for everything to work to our liking. We make rules that

apply only to ourselves and then wonder why
no one else lines up! Even God is flexible. That
is why there is mercy and grace, to fill in for us
when we fail. He made a way to make it easier
for us to please Him.

Locked into the traditional ways of doing things, this
woman at the well was set free when Jesus offered an easier
alternative to worshipping God, to finding the love and
acceptance she so deeply craved. This is something we
should do for others and ourselves. Be open to the new possibilities of finding love and fulfillment in unexpected
places. In every moment of every day, the love we seek is
looking for us. It is a two-way treasure hunt. But we will
miss these hidden treasures if we don't look at the map. The
journey is a simple one because it points straight to the heart
of God, which is ultimately larger and greater than what you
have been looking for. It holds many rivers and tributaries
of refreshing that not only promise to fulfill but also deliver.

4. Know what you have to offer
and give unconditionally.

The standing rule on how to get what you want
is to give it. It is more blessed to give than to
receive because you become the ruler of your
own joy meter! The power to be happy and
feel love, affirmation, and validation, etc., lies
within your own hands and is not contingent
on the behavior or attitude of others.

Our diva at the well made a wonderful discovery in the

midst of her exchange with Jesus. Because she received a revelation of who He was, she now had everything she needed—wholeness and fulfillment. How refreshing! On that note, she left her water pot. She no longer needed it. She had been settling for less than the best for herself. It was merely a temporary fix. Yes, she left the water pot and headed back into town. Toward "the men." The men who had, up to this moment, defined her. The men who had been a source of pain and perhaps even self-loathing. Toward the very people she had been avoiding to give what she had received. It was no longer important to her what their response would be. A passion she had never felt before drove her to give, to pour out what had been imparted to her. And they followed her because passion and love are powerful magnets that can only attract sentiments of like kind. They followed her and received from Jesus themselves. She experienced the fulfillment of finally doing and giving something that really mattered. An entire city became evangelized because of this one woman who remains nameless to us, though you'd better believe God knows her name and has taken careful note of her actions. But the greatest personal victory belonged to her. She was free at last. Free to feel love with or without a man. Free to love and allow others to love as they chose to according to their own ability without subtracting anything away from her.

Diva Confession

I will begin to celebrate the fact God has given me everything that I need at salvation (2 Peter 1:3). The degree to which I experience this is up to me. Therefore, I choose to give what I desire to have and watch it increase as I become an open vessel of blessing to others.

Diva Reflections

✳ What is your deepest longing?

✳ What would it take for you to feel you had acquired it?

✳ How much of your answer is reliant on others?

✳ Are your expectations realistic?

✳ Why is this a need in your life?

✳ How will it be a source of blessing to others?

✳ In what ways can you begin to give what you want to receive?

✳ How will this make you feel?

The Divine Bottom Line

A true diva does not rely on others to make her world—she creates her own universe and invites everyone to the party.

The Diva Anointing

*Y*ou can wander through life undefined, and then one day you do something from the heart that makes a world of difference and nothing you've ever done before, or will do afterward, will define you like that one moment in time. We all have that millisecond of significance scheduled on our divine calendar. The one we've been appointed and anointed to fulfill. We won't know the moment until it is upon us and we feel the rush of adrenaline coursing through our veins saying, "Now! You've got to do it now!" Whatever "it" is. "It" will be needed in that moment, and you will know when as long as you stay sensitive to the Holy Spirit. (Read Matthew 26:6-13.)

Behind the Veil

Soundlessly, she moved toward Him not knowing how He would respond, but feeling a deep sense now was the time. Clutching the alabaster vessel to her chest to quiet the beating of her heart, she couldn't help but feel as if something greater than herself was pushing her forward. There was no explanation for feeling what she felt. This sense of foreboding, this sense of great loss, yet hope for a better tomorrow. The closer she got to Jesus, the more she reflected on past moments shared with Him. Life-changing fragments that had transformed her from a naïve little girl into a woman of great faith. Who wouldn't have faith after watching this extraordinary Man raise their brother from the dead? She recalled the despair she and her sister, Martha, felt after the death of their brother, Lazarus. When he first grew ill, they had called Jesus, but He had not come. Three days went by with Lazarus growing worse. In the heat of his fever, he surfaced just long enough to ask if "He" had come yet, and then he drifted away into a sleep from which he would never return until the Messiah came…or so they thought. And then in the midst of their grief, they were told "He" had arrived. Martha bustled out to meet Him immediately, while Mary remained to gather her thoughts. She found herself unable to reconcile why He hadn't come sooner. Why hadn't He come when He could do something? He had healed others. She knew He loved Lazarus. If He had only come earlier, Lazarus would not have died. She heard herself voicing this one resounding sentiment when she finally stood before Him, although it had been her plan to hear the explanation for His delay first. And in the same breath, she knew she had disappointed Him deeply. His eyes said it all. *Mary, I thought you knew Me better than that….All the time you've spent at My feet, under My tutelage, and it's come to this? You were the one, while Martha distracted herself with much business, who hung on My every word, eyes shining with faith. Don't you remember what I told you that day? You had chosen the better part, the things that would remain, that would never be taken from you…the truth of who I am and what I am able to do.*

His lips never moved, but she saw His heart in His eyes

and soundlessly moved away, ashamed at her own lack of faith....She wasn't sure if her own vision had become distorted by her tears or if He was actually weeping too. This deepened her sense of shame more than her immediate sorrow. Then He was moving past her toward the sealed tomb, telling them to move the stone away, calling "Lazarus!" And miracle of miracles, Lazarus came out of the tomb, no longer ill, no longer dead! And Mary thought to herself, *I will never doubt Him again...*

Now, she did not know if she was dreading some impending tragedy for herself or for Him, but it weighed heavily upon her heart as she began to pour the rich oil of spikenard over His head and His feet. His eyes met hers in silent thanks and understanding, encouraging her to pour out her all. The rest of the room, however, did not share His sentiment, finding it a needless and extravagant waste of what could have been the sum of a man's wages for a year. Wouldn't it have been more beneficial if it was donated to charity?

And then He spoke the words that confirmed what she already knew but desperately wanted to ignore. "Leave her," He said. "She has done a good thing. You will not have me with you always and she has done what she could. She has come beforehand to anoint me for my burial. Be sure that wherever this gospel is preached in the whole world, what this woman has done will also be told as a memorial to her." The words penetrated her soul like shards of broken glass embedding themselves in her heart, small slivers of pain at the confirmation He would be leaving her. She forgot the words she needed to remember: "Mary, I am the resurrection and the life." In the moment, all she could do was feel what she felt, and do what she did with no thought of recognition—though on that day it was noted she would be memorialized throughout the ages for her selfless act. Her very heart was poured out along with the oil that day—only the two of them understood why—and that was all that mattered.

SHE COULD HAVE: Given half or a smaller portion of the oil, and it would still have been considered a generous gift even by Jesus' standards. She could have remained within her budget, her comfort zone, ignoring the prompting of her soul that it was crucial in that moment to give everything, whether she understood why or not.

WHAT SEPARATES THE DIVAS FROM THE GIRLS: Sensitivity to the Spirit of God and a willingness to obey Him, although it may cost everything. Some hear but do not obey. Some hesitate and obey when convenient. A true diva knows that missed cues can cost her much in life. Somewhere in the midst of her obedience lies all she hoped for and more, wrapped in God's pleasure that will always surpass what she's chosen to give.

LIFE LESSON: The true search for significance begins and ends at the feet of Jesus where we find the only lasting contribution we can make is an eternal one. It is the gift of ourselves—given unreservedly from the heart, in the right spirit, that leaves its mark in heavenly and earthly history.

But seek first the kingdom of God and His righteousness, and all these things shall be added to you (Matthew 6:33).

A Diva Is as a Diva Does

We are all created with immense purpose. To grow and contribute something of lasting value to the world, to others, and to those we love is our greatest heart cry. It will not be silenced and the pressing question "Who am I and why am I here?" will persist until we find our place and have done something that mattered. Even Jesus did not feel fulfilled until He had completed what He was sent for, telling His disciples after His encounter with the woman at the well, "I have food you know not of. My meat is to do the will of my Father who sent me." He was energized every time He shared with someone and they got it. It fed Him to give light and life to others. There is something that satisfies us more than the food we eat, the trinkets we acquire, or even the accolades some have the good fortune to collect. It is living up to the fullness of our God-given purpose. Knowing it and doing it.

Ah...for many this is where the struggle begins. "Who am I and why am I here?" repeats itself. Perhaps the reason the answer eludes many is because they make it more complicated than it really is. Who you are and why you are here is to be who you are....Oh, now you're really stuck. Let's face it. Mary, Martha's sister, did nothing really earthshaking, did she, and yet Jesus Himself memorialized her! She simply was a woman who loved the Lord and followed the instinctual prompting of her spirit, without even understanding the full implication of what she was doing. And she ended up being renowned for it. So while we seek to be all deep, weighty, and complicated, thinking the more intricate the web we weave the greater a work of art it

appears to be, her example teaches us that perhaps the profound is much more simple than we thought. Making a
lasting difference comes in many surprising ways. In
sharing a cup of tea, or with a conversation you really didn't
give much thought to. The words you spoke may have
rearranged someone's spirit and caused her to do something that changed a life or touched thousands...all from
one encounter from the heart. See, just being who you are
can be impactful. But how do you develop who you are
into someone who has that type of impact without thinking
about it? I believe the life of Mary holds the answers.

1. Develop a listening heart.
This is the only way to develop your spirit. It
is the heart that is in touch with God and
others that develops a dimension of sensitivity
few possess. Learning how to still ourselves
without and within, rising above the clamor of
the day-to-day and the tyranny of the urgent, is
an art in itself. Life is distracting. It can throw
you off your center so easily if you have not
learned how to ground yourself and hear the
still, small voice of God within.

Mary didn't climb Mount Moriah like Elijah and press
through earthquakes, raging winds, or fearsome fire and
compare all these awesome external experiences to the still
small voice that God prefers to utilize. She simply sat at the
feet of Jesus while activity raged all around her. She made
the time to listen even though it appeared to be inconvenient for others not to have her participation in their activi-
ties. It's been said if the devil can't make you bad, he will

make you busy like Martha and cause you to miss "it." Whatever "it" may be at that moment. Perhaps a snippet of information that was the missing piece of the puzzle you needed to solve an issue in your life. Or an encounter that could have opened a greater door for you. Maybe a simple word that could have rearranged everything in your world in a moment.

The woman who learns to walk with a hearing heart and an open spirit has a major advantage over those who only react to the external pressures they receive at any given moment. Practice taking the time to be quiet. Listen more than you speak. You will be surprised what you hear from others, from God, and from yourself. "Be still, and know that I am God" (Psalm 46:10 NIV).

2. Graduate from fear to faith and love.

God is the only one who does not have to earn our trust because He has already proven Himself to be trustworthy, and yet we put Him through the same paces as those who are trapped within an imperfect mortal body. Although Mary heard all that she heard, she still needed Jesus to prove Himself to her personally. Other people's miracles were not enough; she needed her own. So do we.

But let us not be like the Israelites, who developed many bouts of amnesia throughout their history of interaction with God. Always remember. Build a trophy case and fill it with memories of God's faithfulness to you. Draw from it during moments of doubt. He may not have come when you wanted Him, but He was right on time. Trust will save you years of unnecessary anxiety. It is not about when will He show up. It's about what He is doing even in His seeming absence. What does He want you to see? More importantly, what does He want you to be in the midst of your circumstance? Love will give you the strength to patiently wait because you believe the Lover of your soul will never disappoint you.

3. Give of yourself completely.

Love has no budget. It is oblivious to boundaries. It can't help itself. It is compelled to give. And not just what is convenient or comfortable. Love gives everything. Any person of note recorded in history dared not live on the fringes of love. People made their mark because they pressed past the masses who lived and gave conservatively to give everything, to give more than what was convenient or required. It is not enough to just possess love. One must have passion for someone or something. Heights will never be reached without passion to drive you there. And a life lived without passion is a life that will never be lived to the fullest.

Those who allow themselves to want so much yet give so little will always wonder why they did not touch their dreams, why they seemed to dwell in oblivion, chasing the elusive treasure of fulfillment. Many listen to their heads when they should listen to their hearts and listen to their hearts when they should listen to their heads. When you live and walk in the Spirit, you listen to both. You have mastered how to feel, not by the insistence of the flesh, but by the urgings of the Spirit of God within you.

Love does not question when the Spirit moves or ask why. It responds with trusting obedience knowing all that needs to be revealed will be made clear in time. And the rest? Well, leave it to the One who can do something with the information. Mary broke her bank and gave everything when prompted. Her focus was not on herself, it was on one Man. She was rewarded above what she expected— her name being proclaimed throughout time—the ultimate stamp of approval from the One she loved so deeply. Whether you are reaching out to God or someone else who is significant in your life, remember it is only when you give everything unconditionally, no holds barred, that an impression will be made in their spirit, prompting them to respond to you authentically. Because it is only in that moment they see you as you truly are—a loving and generous woman…a woman to be noted.

Diva Confession

I will listen and learn to trust God's voice. I will purposefully and passionately give my all in obedience to His prompting, knowing wherever He leads me, I will have the awesome privilege of being His partner in divine purpose.

Diva Reflections

✳ How well do you listen?

✳ What keeps you from giving your all in any given situation?

✳ What rewards are you seeking for what you give?

✳ If you never received acknowledgment of what you had done or given, how would you feel?

✳ Why is acknowledgment important to you?

✳ What do you gain from it?

✳ What keeps you from trusting enough to give everything to those you love?

✳ Do you really trust God to be the protector of your heart?

The Divine Bottom Line

A heart that answers the inner call to give its all in a moment when your actions or words will prove crucial makes a significant impact in a person's ordained space, leaving an indelible mark in time that will never be erased.

The Diva Touch

*J*ust when you settle into taking life for granted
something happens to remind you your security
can be a fleeting thing when confronted with issues
that seem larger than you. The unexpected occurrence that
throws your plans awry. The misunderstanding that didn't
get resolved. Someone else's agenda that has nothing to do
with you except, oh my, you happen to be in the way. Any
number of things that rise up in the course of a day to throw
us off kilter and make us throw our hands up and run for
cover. What does a diva do when she feels surrounded?
Attacked? Overwhelmed? Besieged from every side by
family or friends or peers in the workplace? Is it possible to
be heard above the clamor of others' opinions and agendas
or even the beating of your own heart? How do you make
peace when others are intent on war? Every diva must have
a strategy for rising above the fray. Take it from a wise
woman who hung out on a wall. (Read 2 Samuel 20:15-22.)

Behind the Veil

She was a woman like every other woman in Israel. Her
day started the same—rising early and doing the perfunc-
tory tasks that set the day in motion. Nothing foretold the

events that would unfold that day. The women drawing water discussed the same issues they had the day before. The same smells filled the air, the children played the same noisy games, the merchants in the market still haggled as furiously as they ever had. But then the air changed. Tension cut through the languid order of the afternoon. Birds suddenly fluttered restlessly, indicating there was something to be concerned about. With building alarm, the town folk huddled and murmured among themselves. Why was an army gathering at their front door? Why were they battering against the walls that fortified their city? What had they done? This was a safe, peaceful haven. Weren't they the ones everyone came to in order to settle disputes? How did they now find themselves in the midst of a war they knew nothing of? Theirs was a reputation that was spotless among Israel!

She stood listening to the growing panic around her and quietly made a decision. Surely nothing would be solved in the midst of this mayhem. Attempting to guess the other person's motives for this vicious attack would not supply truthful answers. *Better to go to the source than die in the midst of speculation,* she thought. And so she turned her back on the hysteria that surrounded her, making her way to the wall. The wall that now thundered from the sound of the battering it was receiving. Purposely taking deep breaths to calm herself as she climbed the stairs to reach the top, she concentrated intently as slivers of mortar gave way beneath her feet, splattering to the ground that waited to receive her should she fall. Peering over the top of the wall, she surveyed the army below and searched for their leader. She would not waste her words appealing to those who had no power to right the situation. Her eyes picked him out of the crowd—he looked fearsome and determined. He was a man on a mission. Even though she knew the unspoken rule that this was a man's world, she decided it was time for a woman to have her say.

Drinking deep from a reservoir of courage she did not know she had, she called for him, "Please, I would like to speak to Joab, come near so that I may speak to you…" As the man drew near with a bemused expression crossing his otherwise stolid countenance, she continued, "Listen to me your maidservant." "I am listening," he answered. After all, how could he ignore such a humble request? The woman continued, "They used to talk in former times, saying that Abel was the place where others would seek guidance and disputes would be ended. I am among the peaceful and faithful here. You seek to destroy a city and a mother in Israel. Why would you do such a thing?" She prayed she had not spoken out of turn, holding her breath, waiting for his answer. Joab, this leader of King David's army, furrowed his brow causing momentary alarm in her until his words put her fears to rest. He did not want to destroy the city. He was merely in search of a rebel named Sheba who had sought refuge behind their walls. If he were handed over, the army would be on its way.

She could literally feel the fear drain from her body and her courage return. This was simpler than she thought. After all, she lived among people of reason. She felt taller as she stretched to her full stature, and made a simple promise in full assurance of its delivery. "You watch, his head will be thrown to you over the wall." With that she disappeared back into the bowels of her city, heading toward her people. Silencing their suppositions, this nameless woman became known for her wisdom as she delivered the truth of the matter to all who listened, citing this intrusion that endangered them all. Short work was made of an overwhelming problem. The culprit was sought out, beheaded, and sent sailing over the wall. As Sheba's head landed at the feet of the waiting army, Joab signaled the retreat sign, blew the trumpet, and every man withdrew and returned peaceably to his own tent. A sigh that had been withheld as an entire city pondered their fate was released and peace was restored.

SHE COULD HAVE: Gotten caught up in the fear that quickly became contagious within the city, become paralyzed by it, and resigned herself to being part of the populace who would be overrun by the troops who sat outside her community's door.

WHAT SEPARATES THE DIVAS FROM THE GIRLS: Wisdom and courage. A lethal combination in the heart of the right woman. Contrary to popular opinion, sense is not common. To utilize the sense that God gives is a choice, and His wisdom must be sought daily for every circumstance. This diva kept her head while everyone else was losing theirs. She went about the business of solving the problem. It would never be said that she perished without giving her all to avert destruction.

LIFE LESSON: In the midst of a man's world, a woman's touch mingled with wisdom can be a greater force to be reckoned with than natural strength, putting the enemy to flight and deterring impending disaster.

The path of life leads upward for the wise to keep him from going down to the grave (Proverbs 15:24 NIV).

What a Diva Wants, a Diva Gets—and How!

It would be far too simple to summarize great female accomplishments by saying, "All in a day's work for a woman." Yet it is true. A woman can turn the tide of history in a day depending on how she approaches her present circumstances. But how do we, as women seeking to be heard in a society that makes us feel powerless, exercise the type of influence that saves our families, our cities, our nation? Can one woman really make such a huge difference?

Who was this nameless woman found in the twentieth chapter of Second Samuel beginning at the sixteenth verse? We have no clue. She seems to rise from obscurity in the midst of mayhem. While everyone was losing their composure, she maintained hers and actively sought a solution in a very simplistic fashion. Reminding me of a sweet church mother, "Mother So and So" quietly went about solving what could have been a crisis of mammoth proportions.

How do we translate her actions into lessons that work for us where we presently live in order to negotiate our way through the sometimes overwhelming circumstances that press against us on a daily basis? How do we answer those who challenge us in a way that causes us to question if we can achieve the results we are after while maintaining a feminine stance? I believe "Mother So and So" proves to us we can indeed be just as effective, if not more so, than men in the face of conditions that threaten to rob us of the peace, security, and results we desire by utilizing a few simple principles. Let's study them one by one.

1. Seek wisdom over rationalizations.

Never assume anything. It will only incite the other person to excitement or wrath—neither state being desirable when trying to negotiate. Wisdom rises above the fray and allows you a better vantage point in the exchange. Wisdom also leaves room for creative problem-solving. It is better to solve the problem than to be right. Sometimes standing on principle can make us lose more than we know. Leaving room for others to rise to the occasion and do the right thing is powerful. It is better to empower than to forcibly take power for yourself. Wisdom can be contagious. You can't argue with wisdom. To do so would make you look foolish. If we are filled with faith, we can calmly state our case as well as make inquiries that can furnish us with the information needed to make clear judgment calls and solve our dilemma without stress or drama. True divas observe and diffuse dramas; they do not actively participate in them.

Though the story we are gleaning from called for an immediate action, rest assured wisdom takes its time. The first rule in business is: The one who speaks first loses. Sometimes wisdom waits. It lays its cards on the table and waits for the other person to see reason. Wisdom knows it can only deliver the mail, it can't force the recipient to read it or follow the printed directions. But there is a grace to wisdom that usually frees the other person involved to be liberated to do the right thing, unless that person is a fool out and out. In that case, no matter what you do, she or he will be irrational and you, being the wise one, must know the difference. You need to keep in mind who you are dealing with and when to cut your losses.

Never be afraid to admit what wisdom you lack and then seek it. There is safety in a multitude of counselors. When in doubt, surround yourself with the wise. Be brutally honest about your situation, and then be humble enough to receive their counsel and act on it. Wisdom never moves blindly—it walks in the company of understanding and faith. The first thing said about this nameless woman on the wall, "Mother So and So," was she was a wise woman. Certainly wiser than anyone else around her as she is the only one recorded as actively seeking out a solution to end the siege of her city. At the end of the day, let's face it—wisdom always has her way.

2. Put faith before fear.

Trust me. You have not been given the spirit of fear. God has given you a spirit of power, love, and sound mind (2 Timothy 1:7). Only a sound mind accompanied by love and the presence of God in your life can be calm enough to make good decisions. Any decision made in fear will be the wrong one. Panic throws reason to the wind, and the consequences remain long after the storm has ended. Remember, nothing is ever as it seems. Regardless of what you may have experienced in the past, *this* does not mean *that*. Never jump to conclusions. Always seek the truth and root of the matter before summarizing the present circumstance. Respond only after having all the details. Check all your facts.

It is the hidden information that will give you the leverage you need to get your point across effectively and save the day. While the rest of the city huddled and shuddered, "Mother So and So" made her way to the edge of town to ask the leader of the army why he chose to attack them. What better way of finding out? She chose an offensive position rather than a defensive one because she didn't have enough information to defend herself. Or to even know if she needed to! Faith leaves room for seeking understanding because it knows the greatest thing we can ever fear is the unknown. So why not seek enlightenment? It is both unfair and unwise to define someone else's reaction or response according to your own interpretation. Why? Because each of us plays by different internal rules. What upsets me might not upset you. What upsets you may not upset me. If, however, you choose to interpret my upset based on your criteria for being upset, you will then try to fix the circumstance from a place devoid of understanding what is motivating my reaction. This could present a bigger problem because it is possible you may add insult to injury if you are dealing with the wrong information. But if you approach the other person from a place of faith that "this is a problem that most definitely can be solved and surely it can't be as awful as it seems," the stage is set for a rational exchange that can lead to healing. "Mother So and So" had no idea why Joab was getting ready to attack her city. The best way to find out? Ask.

3. Know what you bring to the party.

Keep your eye on the positives. Know your position and use it effectively. "Mother So and So" knew her city's reputation. It had been a place known for solving disputes. They had this to their credit, lending hope to their current situation. Insecurity breeds disrespect and contempt. False bravado is as transparent as Saran Wrap so don't try to hide behind it—it merely leaves the scent of blood and the certainty of attack from hungry lions. Take stock of what has carried you through the other circumstances of your life that have attempted to lay siege against you and draw from that. Know who you are and what you possess that the other side may want. Keep your integrity in the midst of the exchange. Think before you make an offer, and never offer what you cannot deliver.

Never press past the red flag in your spirit. A simpler way of saying it is, "When in doubt, don't." Ah, but when at peace, move forward and conquer! If you're really honest, you've been in this place before and gotten through it. If this is a new experience, get excited. You are getting ready to add another skill to your cache that will be profitable to your spirit, as well as your life, in the long run.

Problems are gifts from God to make us grow and keep life exciting. Approaching life as an amazing and interesting game can keep us moving around the board at a steady pace with fewer and fewer detours away from victory—if we choose to learn as we go. "Mother So and So" positioned herself on the wall not just physically, but positionally as well. She made it clear to her opponent who she was, what qualified her to speak to him, and rationally asked for an explanation for his attack. He, being a man of reason, could only respond in the right fashion and be open to another resolution. Physical strength faced mental and spiritual strength and all involved bowed to the better way.

4. Get help when you need it.

Your personal victory will always be a blessing to someone other than yourself; therefore, invite someone else to the party. No need to hoard the credit, just get the task done. Excellence has its own way of gaining recognition. Be a team player—life is not a contest. If we don't win together in the end, we all lose. It's no fun watching from the sidelines. When everyone feels as if she is a part of the victory, all dance together. "Mother So and So" went back into the city and appealed to the people. Collectively, they gathered strength, beheaded, and ousted Sheba, the one who had brought danger to their doorstep.

I'm sure Sheba was a nice guy, at least to them—especially since he was seeking asylum from them; however, he was the problem. He had to be gotten rid of. The town folk understood that evil flourishes when good men do nothing. In spite of their fear, they banded together, and together they delivered their city. I doubt very seriously if this one wise woman ever said, "If it weren't for me…" No, the bigger picture was far more beautiful to look at. Once again they were safe, and peace had been restored.

Diva Confession

In moments when I feel my peace, joy, or security is being threatened, I will not move in anger or fear. Instead, I will utilize the love, faith, and wisdom God affords me to order my steps and conversation toward a positive end.

Diva Reflections

✳ How powerful do you feel as a woman?

✳ What challenges do you face on a daily basis when it comes to being heard in your home? In your work place?

✳ Do you feel as if you are able to make significant contributions to your peers?

✳ How do you present yourself and your gifts to others?

✳ Have you curried a reputation for wisdom or are you struggling to make your place?

✳ In what area have you been weakest?

✳ What personal fears keep you from operating effectively when you feel any area of your life go under siege?

The Divine Bottom Line

Wisdom always wins the war—bloodlessly extracting what is needed from both parties without pointing a finger of accusation at either while seeking peace for both. Wisdom takes no credit for settling the score—it simply seeks to leave everyone involved wiser for the exchange.

Claim Your Destiny

Destiny calls…
challenging us to make choices
we might not
normally make
under the usual circumstances.
But nothing
about this day
is as the others…
without a plan or
specific reason,
merely keeping pace
with where it was being taken
until it was intercepted
by a defining moment
that asked it
of its purpose,
forcing it to
consider the junction
and choose….
The left?
Or the right?
Finally risking the road
less traveled,
hoping to forge
a path all its own
that would take it to higher ground,
giving it a vantage point
to finally
see the big picture…
where the plan of God
would be laid
divinely bare,
and understanding would be attained
once
and for all…

A Diva and Her Choices

I've said it often, "conversations in heaven get us in trouble here on earth. God has a plan for your life." We've heard it time and time again, and indeed He has. He knows the plans He has for us, but sometimes we do not. Here is where things get interesting. Our destiny is laid out unbeknownst to us. Enter stage left the antagonist in this drama called life, whose thoughts toward you are contrary to God's. His plans are for evil not good—to destroy your future and unravel the determined end God has prepared for you—but the accuser needs your help to do it. He needs you to make the wrong choices, and he is happy to serve up just the "right" ones to seduce you off the narrow path.

Can he rob you of your destiny? I think not. To say otherwise would make God less powerful than he, and that is certainly not the case. However, Satan can do a good job of causing needless delay, though God will merely use the time to work something out in you to the greater good because He's in no hurry. Let's face it, He's got all the time in the world. However, it is usually during this juncture we fail to see the big picture and get paralyzed if we don't stay clear on the facts. It's not how quickly the race is run; it's how we finish. Divas who trust in God finish well no matter what wrong turns they may have taken along the way.

57

There are a few things in life that are granted to every person. Two of those would be a destiny and the incredible gift of choice. Sometimes the gift of choice can seem like a curse, depending on how we use it. And who hasn't been guilty of making bad choices? Sometimes voluntarily, sometimes involuntarily. Whether it is something as simple as unwittingly walking down the wrong street and becoming a victim, to purposely making a choice you knew was the wrong one but hoped you wouldn't be right. Some choices are entirely innocent ones while others are blatant acts of rebellion borne out of frustration, anger, fear, unbelief, or impatience. Usually the moment the consequences begin to manifest, we wonder if we'll ever have another chance to do things differently.

"If I coulda, shoulda, woulda," "If only I had...," "What was I thinking?" Shall I go on? Regret can be like a wet blanket cutting off our ability to breathe, to pray, and to hope for a new start, which God always grants. It is at this fork in the road, when we are given the chance to get back on track, that our destiny lies in our hands. To become or not to become what God wants you to be is the headline question. A true diva rises to her highest potential in this defining moment, choosing to redirect her path, knowing that though there is nothing she can do about her past, it does not dictate her future. A new life awaits her the moment she turns her face toward God and heads in His direction. As she continues to be guided by His eyes, He leads her to higher ground.

Divine Dedication

We've all been there. Just as you begin to see light at the end of the tunnel, you are dealt a blow that leaves you feeling winded and forsaken. Where do you go from here now that you find yourself alone, isolated in your circumstance and questioning if you'll ever be able to rely on anyone ever again? You stand at a crossroad. Faith versus fear. Courage versus resignation. It is at this point in the journey that every diva must decide what she really believes and who she really believes in. (Read Luke 8:2; John 19:25; 20:1-18.)

Behind the Veil

She didn't care what anybody thought, said, or did. She was not leaving, not denying Him. It wasn't as if He hadn't warned them. This was what He had been talking about all along. They just didn't understand. Or perhaps they didn't want to. Judas had betrayed Jesus just as He had predicted. And now, as she sat in the courtyard listening to the tone of the crowd, it seemed as if there might not be much hope for His release. This same crowd who had loved Him, seeking His words and His miracles, now was dark, ominous, and threatening—accusing Him of heresy and condemning Him even before He had a trial. The battle lines were clearly drawn, and many of His disciples had already retreated out of fear that they too would be condemned with Him. *Peter, oh Peter, how could you?* she thought. Even Peter had denied Him when questioned about his association with Him.

No, things did not look good. Even as she tried to drum up hope, His words predicting His own death haunted her. It was more than she could bear to think of Him leaving them. She wondered if the voices would return to torment her again in His absence. No! She shook her head as if to shake off the fear that threatened to squeeze the breath from her body. She had been delivered from those evil spirits the moment He touched her. They said seven demons had fled from her. All she knew was her peace had been restored and her agony had ended. From that moment she had followed Him, using her resources, along with the others, to help with supplying provisions as they moved from place to place. Now she was here and would remain by His side to the bitter end. If no one else was there for Him, she would be.

In the days that followed, her pain at times was even deeper than when the demons had tormented by attacking her mind and her body. She convulsed with pain at the agony of His suffering. Her beloved *Rabboni*. Beaten beyond recognition, bloody and bowed, He painfully made His way to Golgotha, where they brutally nailed Him to the cross and left Him to die. And as she watched with His mother and beloved disciple John, the last of His breath ebbed away. She felt as if she had died a million deaths. She had been powerless to save Him who had so graciously saved her. She found it hard to believe He was really gone, even as they took His body down and prepared it for burial. She thought perhaps her insanity was trying to reclaim her as she fought against a deep abiding hope—call it a feeling—this was not the end. He would not leave her or forsake her. But the immediate circumstances yanked her back to reality as they rolled the stone across the entryway of His tomb and sealed it, as if to finalize the fact He was truly gone. And she was left to stand looking at the stone, feeling a gaping hole in the place where the love in His eyes and His gentle words had filled her to overflowing before.

Where can I go now that He's not here? she thought. She might have set up permanent camp by the tomb if it wasn't for the others drawing her away. Yet she was pulled back to it, drawing a strange comfort from being near to it. If this was all that she could have of Him, it would be enough.

Then on the first day of the week, after tossing and turning throughout a sleepless night, she rose while it was still dark and made her way to the tomb—only to find a most unusual sight. The stone had been rolled away! Running to get the other disciples, she could see the speculation in their eyes, the unspoken thought that perhaps she'd had a relapse. Only John and Simon Peter followed when she urged them to come and see. Returning to the tomb with her, they did not know what to make of it. The stone had been rolled away. The linens that covered Jesus' body were neatly folded and left behind... *Where could they have taken him?* Her mind reeled. This was more than she could bear. It was enough to be robbed of His life, but now to be robbed of His presence even as He "slept" was the deepest cruelty. She could control the flow of her tears no longer. She could imagine no deeper pain.

"Woman, why are you weeping?" Her eyes tried to focus on the two strangers before her. "They have taken away my Lord and I do not know where they have laid Him," she answered. Grief-stricken, she turned to encounter yet another stranger who asked, "Woman, why are you weeping? Whom are you seeking?" Her mind rocked as the questions pushed her close to the edge of her last bit of calm. She sought frantically to muster her courage. "Sir, if you have carried Him away, just tell me where you have laid Him and I will take Him away." *Only please do not separate Him from me any longer for I could not bear it.* This she did not say aloud but screamed it silently from the inner recesses of her heart.

And then, as if she were in a dream, He called her name, "Mary." There He was in the flesh standing before her, looking more beautiful than ever to her—Jesus. "Rabboni!" she cried. As she ran to embrace Him, He said to her, "Do not cling to Me for I have not yet ascended to My Father. Go to My brethren and say to them, 'I am ascending to My Father and your Father, and to My God and your God!'" (John 20:17). And so she ran, carrying the good news to the disciples. Jesus had not left them. He had kept His promise. She too would remain ever faithful to carry out His wishes to the end.

SHE COULD HAVE: Bowed to the pressure of the masses and retreated out of fear, denying Him and compromising her faith with the rest of the crew. She could have sunken into self-pity and hopelessness, deciding she would be doomed to being alone and forsaken.

WHAT SEPARATES THE DIVAS FROM THE GIRLS: Unrelenting

devotion that is unshakable in the face of adverse circumstances or moments of question. The facts are
simple. Jesus literally rescued them from hell. Turning
back was not an option. Divas are sold out—faithful fol-
lowers and servants. In the end, Jesus returns the act of
faithfulness, letting them know their faith is not in vain.

LIFE LESSON: Even when we don't understand what God is
doing in our lives, we must remain steadfast. He who is
always faithful will reward our faithfulness if we do not
waver by revealing an even greater aspect of His power
and love for us.

> *But we also glory in tribulations, knowing that
> tribulation produces perseverance; and perse-
> verance, character; and character, hope. Now
> hope does not disappoint, because the love of
> God has been poured out in our hearts by the
> Holy Spirit who was given to us* (Romans 5:3-5).

It's Not What a Diva Knows, But Who...

The easiest way to find out what is valuable to people is
to notice the way they treat that person or thing. Where it
falls on the list of priorities and how much time they commit
to the care of that thing or person is just as important a clue.
Where your treasure is, your heart will be also (Luke 12:34).
What is fought for is appreciated more than what is gained
with no struggle. It is from a heart of gratitude that true
commitment comes. But every commitment must be tested,
tried in the fire, and refined to even greater strength.

Commitment that passes the test of time and trials reaps its own reward in the end, although many may not understand it along the way. Only the heart that fervently beats for what it is committed to understands that the root of it goes beyond gratefulness to a deep abiding love. Mary Magdalene loved Jesus and not just for what He had done for her. She loved Him for who He was. She went beyond the gift to the giver, securing her place in His heart, as well as in the center of her God-given destiny. Every diva who fulfills her destiny is driven by a heart that beats for what she is committed to. As she seeks to fulfill her calling, the journey keeps her from falling. Where does that type of commitment come from? From choices that become personal rituals along the way.

1. Remember what you've been delivered from.

Don't regret your past—simply remember it in the right light. After you've made the decision to accept the wholeness that God offers, embrace the lessons from the pain you've experienced in the past and use them as fuel to move forward. It is because of your unique experiences that you can be used to effectively contribute to the greater plan of blessing others around you.

You are a prime candidate to be used as a vessel of blessing to someone. Your past holds the key to your destiny. It's been said that it is our flaws that make us interesting—our brokenness, past mistakes, and failings. Now you know sisters can have some issues, but God is able to take them all and make something beautiful out of them. It's called character.

The demons that threatened your belief in what you had to offer, what God was able to do for you and through you and what the future holds for you, can only be silenced when you agree with God about your destiny, which is to bring pleasure to God and glorify Him in a way that blesses others. This can happen in many ways. It can range from something as simple as listening to someone who feels isolated and hopeless to something as complicated as starting a movement that frees a nation of people from oppression. The effects of one small act can have major ramifications throughout generations. Whatever it is...take the healing, the deliverance, the liberty God has given you and use it.

Take the comfort you have been comforted with and extend it to others. And by all means, forget the parts that kept you paralyzed. Remember just enough to never want to return to where you were. Remember just enough to want to keep others from traveling the same road.

Destiny is not about acquiring greatness for your name's sake. That is why initial perfection or greatness is not required for achieving it. Destiny is about fulfilling your call—contributing to the world what you were created to give—which could be one word on a given day or a more profound action. The ripple effect will set things in motion, moving us all closer to our collective destiny—that is living up to our calling and completing our divine assignment.

2. Nurture a grateful heart.

It is not the regret we feel toward the past, or even the questions why that should consume our time, but gratefulness to God for what we have survived and overcome.

A grateful heart comes from the recognition of God's mercy and grace being manifested in your life. No matter what state you're in, God sees you as a completed work. By His Spirit, we must embrace His vision and joyfully expect Him to finish the work He has started in us.

Taking stock on where we are versus where we've been should truly be reason enough to celebrate. Build your faith trophy case, and admire the things you place there. For example, the time God defied the doctor's report and healed you. The time He restored you from financial devastation. The time He caressed your broken heart and brought it back to life. Look back and ponder how you got over the wall. God is *good*...all the time. Actually, we all know He is better than that. He is unspeakable and full of glory. We just don't give Him the just desserts He deserves.

If it is hard to make sense of where you've been and what has happened to you, consider this: God knew you would make it. He knew you would be strong enough to overcome and turn that experience around for good by now being equipped to minister to someone who needs your help in overcoming the same trial. Did He deliberately inflict your suffering on you? No. That's not His department. However, in His foreknowledge of the events, He allowed it to happen and made provision for you to get through it, overcome, and flourish because of it. You were not created to simply survive. You were created to thrive and make a lasting contribution to others in your world.

Consider your wounds badges of honor instead of causes to grow bitter and feel forsaken. Nothing could be further from the truth. God is nearer than you think, fully acquainted with your suffering. Don't grow bitter, grow better as I always say. Success is the best revenge against the things that have assaulted you. Rise above them and use them. Allow them to inspire greater praise and worship. Paul said he counted it a privilege to be counted worthy to suffer with Christ. Not everyone shares this noble sentiment. Some folks just fold and die if the wind blows too hard. They are not a threat to the kingdom of darkness so the enemy of our souls doesn't give them a backward glance. Ah, but you my sister must be a triple threat if you've been keeping on. Don't wonder why, just get excited! God has amazing plans for you. Praise Him for putting His confidence in you as a warrior who can be counted on. In all things, praise Him. Thank Him that the situation is not worse. Thank Him that He sees you and is working it out for your good even if you can't see the outcome. Thank Him because even if you don't know the specifics of the matter, you know one thing—in the end you win. And for that you can be truly grateful.

3. Choose to serve someone.

If you don't use your trials to get to the next level, you lose. Use them to help someone. It's called getting over yourself. The interesting thing about pain is you only feel it when you are focused on yourself. If you are distracted by the needs of others, though the pain may be very real and exist, it won't be as devastating because your attention is elsewhere. Mark this as a fact. You have been called to use all that you've suffered as a manual to serve somebody. It is in the pouring out of yourself to others that true healing comes to you. Nothing will ever make you feel more alive than growing in your circumstances and contributing what you've learned to the care and betterment of others.

The world at-large is self-consumed for the most part, thriving on instant gratification in all forms. While people rush to and fro looking for yet another experience or trinket that will give them a greater feeling of satisfaction, the point is missed. It is not what you do for yourself that fills you up. It is what you do for others. Mary recognized that Jesus had done something no one else could do for her, and she wanted to return the favor by serving Him wholeheartedly. She chose to follow Him and be there for Him. She counted it a privilege to serve the One who had served her, knowing her service to Him enabled Him to serve others.

Today the thought of serving someone is considered beneath the average person. You might think there is no glamour in servanthood if you lack understanding on the power of it. And yet Jesus Himself was the greatest example of servant leadership. He was the One who cooked for and served the disciples. He washed their feet! He nurtured them as well as led them. Contrary to popular belief, the way up is down. You cannot lead those you have not served. No one follows someone they are forced to surrender to. They follow those who serve their needs.

I believe I am where I am today because of the time I spent serving a cousin of mine in the ministry. From what would be considered the most menial and inconsequential of tasks to the more glamorous, I counted it a privilege to serve such a great vessel of God. I wanted to learn from him. I, like Elisha following after Elijah to get his anointing, went the extra mile to be a blessing to him. I did it for *no pay* and felt that what I learned was payment above and beyond what I could receive. Today, I can truly say that God honored my time, commitment, and sacrifice by blessing me with the opportunity to serve you and others. At the end of the day, if I've made a difference in the life of one, then I feel I've done my job.

Feeling bored? Feeling empty? Feeling life owes you more of something you can or can't put your finger on? Find someone to serve and watch your heart begin to fill up and become full with a fulfillment you didn't know was possible. (I like that—being fully filled.) Perhaps you say, "I'm still too broken myself to reach out to someone else." That's the best time to do it. Reach past your own pain and disappointment to bring joy and healing to someone else and find yourself miraculously filled with what you've been looking for yourself. That is the power and the glory of servanthood.

4. Be more committed to your future than you were bound to your past.

Deliverance from your past will not take place until you replace what you got rid of with something more pleasurable. Something that will keep you from returning to whence you came. Commit yourself to transformation and lasting change. Take a realistic look at where you were and what it cost you, and willfully decide never to allow yourself to be robbed that way again. Select a new direction of focus, one that will bring rewards to your life spiritually, physically, or emotionally, and apply yourself to it with all your heart.

Whether you believe it or not, we *do* get to choose—life or death, blessings or curses—every day of our lives. God has given us that kind of power. Either we don't believe it or we take it for granted. Now is the time to take your life back and run with it. Mary was bound with seven demons before she met Christ. That number seven is very significant. It speaks of completion. She was completely taken over by whatever it was that plagued her. We do not know what the demonic manifestation was, whether it was something of an epileptic nature, deep depression—we don't know. Though the popular school of thought is that she was a woman of ill repute, there is no biblical or historical support for that. Obviously she was a woman of means because she supported Jesus' ministry not only with her time, but financially as well. I do not believe He would have accepted ill-gotten gain. Which brings me to the point that once she was freed of her infirmity, she was completely given over to following and serving Christ regardless of what it cost her. This is why she could be fearless even when the other disciples had fled. She had nowhere else to go. There was no going back. No other feasible alternative.

We must be just as sold out to the new direction we take as she was. We need to leave behind the bondage, the people, and the things that hinder us once and for all.

As you consider what you have been delivered from, you get the opportunity to flip the script and turn your trials around for the good. The man or woman who is forgiven of much loves much the Bible tells us. But what about you? How will you show your gratitude to God for what He's brought you through? To those who have assisted or blessed you along the way? Will you allow negative experiences to sap you of your strength or cause you to give less of yourself the next time around? Bondage was not your choice, but freedom is. Exercise your freedom to give from a generous heart. There is nothing to fear. Your choice to give exempts you from robbery. Jesus laid down His life; no one took it from Him. You can only be robbed of what you refuse to let go of. When you choose to give, choose to live, choose to love, and serve with all your heart, mind, soul, and strength you will be empowered to walk in a liberty you could only imagine before.

Diva Confession

I will not allow myself to be bound by my former circumstances. Instead, I will embrace my deliverance with a grateful heart. In moving forward, I will take the parts I can use from my former experience and transform them into tools I can use to bless others.

Diva Reflections

✴ What has kept you from living the life you've wanted to live so far?

✴ How do these things keep you from moving forward?

✴ What is the false belief concerning your circumstance?

✴ What is the truth?

✴ What keeps you from moving beyond this way of thinking?

✴ What new belief can you adopt to help you move past where you are?

✴ What can you be grateful for right now?

✴ Who can you serve right now?

✴ What new thing can you commit to today to get you on your way to the fulfillment you long for?

The Divine Bottom Line

It is only when we are broken and crushed that the fragrance of our lives can become an offering that can enhance and bless others.

Divine Restoration

We've all made bad choices. We get caught up in the moment. We do something that has lasting consequences. We unthinkingly get trapped in fleeting passion. The remains of the day, second, or hour is more than we thought it would ever be. Unplanned changes throw our lives off kilter, and we wonder if we will ever find our rhythm again. How will we live with the opinions of our peers when this outcome cannot be hidden? How will we find restoration? In times like these, the grace of God remains, giving us the strength we need to make the right choices and to get on with the business of rising above our circumstances and overcoming the odds. (Read 2 Samuel 11:1–12:24.)

Behind the Veil

Bathsheba stretched, allowing the air to wrap around her like a warm blanket. Languishing in the feel of the water pouring over her body like liquid fingers cleansing and gently massaging her limbs, she reveled in this time of purification. From her perch on the roof, she truly felt above all the affairs of the day. She thought of her husband, Uriah, strong and brave, away at battle, and wondered how he fared. For a moment, she almost felt guilty for feeling so free, so relaxed while he faced such danger. Her thoughts were interrupted by a feeling...a feeling she was being watched. But who could it be? All the houses were either on the same level or slightly beneath hers. Most people in her neighborhood utilized their rooftops as much as they did the rest of the house. Turning ever so slightly, her eyes came to rest on the palace that rose above all the homes in the area. Thinking she saw a movement, she turned fully to get a better look, but saw no one. Not being able to shake the feeling, she covered herself and descended the stairway leading back to solid ground. Perhaps being alone so long was beginning to play tricks on her mind and make her paranoid. She prayed Uriah would return home soon. She was lonely.

Shortly after eating her dinner, the knock came. Sharp and authoritative. A sense of foreboding churned within her as she made her way to the door. One of the king's guards stood before her, and instantly she clutched her hands to her chest. Was it Uriah? What had gone wrong? Was he all right? But this had nothing to do with her husband. The king had requested an audience with her. *With me? What could he possibly want? Well perhaps he wanted to give her news concerning Uriah...* But why wouldn't the king just send someone to relay the message? Her mind was jumbled as she followed the guard, whose face gave no hint of what this could be all about.

And then she was there. Standing before him, thinking he was even more handsome close up than the glimpses she had been able to gather of him from afar during pro-cessionals. She had not been privy to his dance through the streets with the ark, literally celebrating himself right out of his clothes as the women still loved to discuss. As she bowed before him, he seemed taller, larger than life. She waited, but still no word of Uriah, only an invitation to dine with him. This heightened her confusion as she waited to discover the reason for this unusual summons. He seemed a bit too relaxed and social to be calling her for urgent business. She had heard of his wide-ranging taste in women, but she would not allow her thoughts to go any further down that road. Surely he knew she was the wife of Uriah.

She had already eaten, but how do you say no to a king? Lightly tasting the sumptuous fare presented to her, she waited for the purpose of her visit to be revealed. She had to admit that he was rather charming, and when he leaned toward her, she was disturbed by what she felt. Perhaps Uriah had been gone too long. She chided herself, trying to stave off the inappropriate thoughts and feelings that were washing over her in waves. It seemed as if he were moving closer and closer to her. Was it her imagination or wishful thinking? It was hard for her to separate her thoughts with any sense of clarity when he touched her and ever so lightly began to caress her.

A myriad of thoughts swirled in her head. She felt as though she were fighting to keep her head above water. Water that was slowly and forcefully taking her under its spell. The law came to mind. She should push him away. She should cry for help. It was the only chance she had at maintaining her innocence. But he was the king. How do you accuse the king of rape? And was it really? Perhaps she had unwittingly played some part in this. Perhaps she had wanted him just as badly as he wanted her. But it was so wrong. It was so wrong...

As she made her way back home in the corners of the night, she prayed fervently although she could not remember for what. Even if he never called her again, it would never be over. Though she thought she saw traces of regret in his eyes afterward and he had gently sent her away, she knew they both would be haunted by this night forever. Why couldn't Uriah be like every other husband who simply worked and stayed at home? Why did he have to be so passionate about being a soldier? It was all his fault. His absence had put her in this position. No, it was David's fault. Just because he was king did not mean he could take whom he pleased. He certainly did not live above God's law even though he chose to live above his own. Perhaps it was her fault. Had she invited his lust by bathing on the rooftop? No, it was where she always bathed. She and countless other women in Israel. Whether she was a victim or a volunteer for what had occurred she could not decide. God help me. Forgive both of us...

Weeks passed and the dread within her stomach grew into a ball of conception. She knew it! It would have been far too simple for life to overlook the events of that night and tuck them beneath the stars where they belonged among the only silent witnesses who would keep such a secret. But now the light of day and the accuracy of time would broadcast their dalliance in clear view. She sent a simple message to him while wondering how he would choose to solve this dilemma. After all, he was the king was he not? "I am with child," it stated. The ball was now in his court.

Uriah was beckoned from the war. She was not sure if that was the solution she was seeking because she did not know how she could face him without him looking into her soul and seeing the truth. But dear Uriah, she should have known that should be the least of her fears. He refused to come to her bed, citing he could not enjoy the comforts of home while his fellow soldiers fought. How could she tell him that being principled at a time like this could do them more harm than good without betraying herself and her actions to him? She waited for the other shoe to drop.

And drop it did. Sending Uriah back to the battlefield carrying his own death sentence in a note to Joab, he sealed his fate with his sense of honor. The word came as she rested one afternoon, already feeling the effects of her pregnancy. Uriah was dead. Killed in the heat of battle. Now what? She descended into her mourning, not being able to separate who she was really grieving for—herself or Uriah. As her period of bereavement came to a close, a knock came at the door again. She was to join David in the palace as his wife.

Before she could even question what or how or why, she found herself facing David, his face even more gentle than before, reassuring her everything would be all right. He would take care of her and protect her. Perhaps that was true of the outside world, but nothing could protect her from the eyes of the women of the court and the palace intrigue that raged after her arrival. None would dare say a word openly about what they perceived. Nathan the prophet came, boldly confronting David in the presence of all who could hear it. Though God forgave David the moment he repented, He would not excuse them from the consequences. The child would die.

How much death am I to bear? Bathsheba wondered. Her husband, her baby, her life as she had known it ebbed away as she watched this small beauty breathe its last breath. And then David was there. After fasting and praying before the Lord, he had chosen to wash himself and comfort her. It seemed in the midst of their suffering a bond had formed that would never be broken. Though many would never understand how she came to claim his heart, she knew it was an act of grace from God that bound him to her and restored the life she thought she had lost.

A lifetime-and-a-half later, Bathsheba looked upon her dying husband David. No longer a naïve young woman but a seasoned veteran of kingdom living and the wise mother of four sons, she stood before him and gently reminded him of his promise to pass the crown to Solomon, her eldest son. He was ready. She had purposed in her heart from the beginning to teach him wisdom from the things she had learned, as well as the mistakes she had made. To instill in him principles that would cause him to walk in favor with God and with man. He had been a bright and willing student, surpassing her expectations. Now the day had come. It seemed as if only yesterday David had sent for her. They had weathered much together. Open shame, uprisings, rebellions, disgrace, family dysfunction, but nothing had displaced their love and trust for one another. In a moment, her friend would be leaving her and taking the secrets they were able to keep with him. She resolved, as she gazed upon her son, her work on earth was not yet done.

SHE COULD HAVE: Become hysterical from the unfolding events that seemed beyond her control and chosen to be a victim rather than a victor in her circumstance.

WHAT SEPARATES THE DIVAS FROM THE GIRLS: The true diva has the ability to live and flourish in spite of the trials that threaten to rob her of the life she had imagined. The ability to exercise prudence and discretion when it is crucial to her very existence and make her trial work *for* her instead of against her, emerging the better for it.

LIFE LESSON: Self-pity is a foe not an ally. In order to reclaim the broken pieces of your life, as well as the things you feel you've lost, you must willfully rise above the disappointment and questions that can flood your being. Chart a new course on the map you've been handed, believing you can still reach a destination called victory.

Many are the afflictions of the righteous, but the Lord delivers them out of them all (Psalm 34:19).

Divas Get Over It and Get On with It

I watched the woman and sensed her fresh pain as she recounted her rape more than 20 years earlier as if it had happened yesterday. As the conference leader brought to light the fact that no cell in her body that was present then was present now, citing the scientific reality that every part of our being is regenerated within a two-year period, he asked her what was stopping her from getting past it. "It's still in my head," she said. When asked what it had cost her to cling to the memory, she replied, "Everything." She found it difficult to have quality relationships with anyone. She was fearful and distrustful, awaiting the next personal violation. She was an unhappy recluse, bound in her own personal prison.

We will never know if Bathsheba was raped or gave herself willingly to David, but we can all agree the fallout that happened afterward was no picnic. Disgrace, shame, loss, and countless regrets hung over them for the rest of their lives. Though granted reprieves of happiness along the way, a word spoken, an unconscious action, or even something unthinkingly jested brought back memories of a time when life was more tenuous and agonizing.

While some have suffered because they were taken against their will, countless others have given themselves willingly only to feel just as violated in the end. The remains of these encounters serve as constant reminders of the pain and disappointment experienced. How does one move on? Perhaps your situation is not one of a sexual nature, but you've made mistakes that have cost you just as much or more, whether emotionally, financially, physically, or spiritually. An impulsive action or word that cost you everything invited such unexpected ramifications you were left wondering if you'd ever recover, ever smile, ever enjoy the life you were living, ever love, or ever laugh again. How do you turn consequences into a blessing? How do you get the life back you lost? How do you keep moving when you want to die? What do you do when you can't find the off button for the pain? Bathsheba and David give us several clues to moving forward.

1. Forgive yourself.

Forgive your offender or the participant in your situation. Repent of your part in the script if you must. Accept God's forgiveness and, by all means, forgive yourself. Your destiny awaits. A lot of time can be wasted chastising yourself. "If only…" has been sung a thousand different ways, and no one has come up with the answer on how things would have worked out differently. Stop beating yourself up. Condemnation does not come from God; it comes from the accuser of your soul. The moment you asked God to forgive you He did and moved on. He flung your deed into the sea of forgetfulness, and He is not going fishing anytime soon.

The difficult thing about forgiving yourself that you must understand is that guilt is a function of the spirit, not the intellect. This is why countless dollars are wasted on psychologists. As they try to help you justify your actions, peace eludes you. The quickest way to settle the debt with yourself is to own it and discard it like the garbage that it is. "Yes, I did contribute to my situation." Whether it was being in the wrong place when "something" told you not to go there or whatever the "failing" may be. The next step is to put guilt in its place. "I made a mistake, but Christ died for my mistakes and misdeeds; therefore, I will accept His forgiveness and will not return to this place again." Release yourself as God has released you to begin again.

Now, don't claim guilt if it is not yours to own. For example, the abused woman who feels she somehow was responsible for her beating. Perhaps the only part she plays in that case is continuing to remain with a man she knows has violent tendencies. There is never a justification for abuse. For the most part, listen to your spirit, which echoes God's heart, and follow it.

2. Grieve.

Go ahead, feel the pain. Weep if you want. Acknowledge something has died even if it is just a dream of how your life was supposed to go. Tears have a way of cleansing the soul and refreshing the spirit. As you release all that is bottled up inside, God collects those precious tears in a bottle and does not disregard one (Psalm 56:8).

Mourn what you have lost. Accept the fact in the midst of grieving that you are acknowledging the end of something. The end in this case simply means the end of that particular chapter. Not the end of the book or journey. Make peace with that fact, and purpose to anticipate the next chapter or turn. There is always the chance for a new beginning if we keep hope in view. Clear your slate, and prepare yourself to move forward. Grieving does not give you a license to live in the past. It is the winter of your soul, shedding the old to make way for spring, when things that appeared dead begin to bloom again and fill the earth with vivid colors and aromatic scents. If not for winter, we would not appreciate spring and notice the difference between seasons. Grief, too, is a season, so plant new seeds of expectation, decide how you want your garden to grow, and water it with your tears. Make sure you dry your eyes in time to see and enjoy the first blooms.

3. Take control of what you can and move forward.

Lay aside anything that keeps you from moving forward, but remember as much as you need to propel yourself to the next level. I believe David had the right idea after the death of his son. There was no more need to dwell on it. Nothing would change. He mourned for him while he thought there was a chance to reverse the outcome of the situation, but after the child's death, the best way to honor him was to go on living with fond memories of the little time they had with him.

What can you control about your situation? You can control your attitude, which will rule your actions, which will affect the outcome of your circumstance. You felt out of control when your situation happened? Well now it's your turn to take it back. Will you live in fear, regret, shame, resignation, and bitterness forever? Or will you thrive in spite of everything and everyone associated with your pain and disappointment? The choice is yours.

Second, you get to decide how you move on and make the situation worth everything you went through. Here is where you get to empower yourself. Here is where you get the opportunity to squeeze something out of your pain that could work for you. Let the things that could have bound you make you more sensitive to the needs of others.

Decrease in judgment and increase in empathy. This is your chance to be like Jesus, who because He suffered is able to sympathize with us. So it is in this relating that we are effective in delivering those we reach out to. Ultimately, our collective destiny, though some will be singled out for greatness in this endeavor, is to heal and deliver others. The most effective conduits of this awesome gift are those who have been through something themselves.

4. Learn your lessons, and teach them to others.

Truly our mess becomes our ministry, our test becomes our testimony. Still wondering why you are here? Consider your own life. Your own struggles. In the midst of personal trials is where you will find the key to unlock the door to fulfilling your purpose, especially if it is a recurring theme. Don't miss it. Always remember that if the enemy of your soul felt he had to throw that great a wrench into your path to get you off course, you need to hightail it back on track. Obviously you were on your way to a tremendous blessing he didn't want you to have. Get back in the race and see.

Consider what lessons there are to learn from your experience. Embrace them and mold them into tools that will not only help you to help yourself, but others as well. At the end of the day, Bathsheba took her life experiences and tutored her son to greatness. She contributed to the Book of Proverbs, telling Solomon bits of wisdom that would serve him well in life along with *maaajor* lessons on the type of wife he should look for! As a matter of fact, she had a lot to say to him on the topic of women and how they could ultimately affect his life. The greatest lessons in life come from those who have the scars to show for a war well fought along with their victories.

Diva Confession

I will not allow myself to be a victim of my past. In spite of my failings, mistakes, or even the violation of others, I will thrive and flourish, becoming all I was created to be—a woman under grace, imparting the same to others.

Diva Reflections

✳ What circumstances have occurred in your life in which you felt powerless or out of control?

✳ What was your response?

✳ What were the consequences that followed?

✳ How did you handle the outcome?

✳ In hindsight, what would you have done differently?

✳ Would it have made a difference? How?

✴ In light of present reality, how can you move forward in a way that is healthy and constructive?

✴ What steps will you take immediately to get on track for victory?

✴ What lessons have come out of this for you?

✴ What would you say to others in the same situation?

The Divine Bottom Line

For every broken thing that's ever been mended, a stronger vessel stands in its place—now capable of holding more, standing firmer, and enduring longer. The true beauty of a broken vessel is its uniqueness—no two can be broken alike. It is that brokenness that makes it more precious to its owner, the only one who truly knows where the flaw lies and the value that comes from the markings.

Divine Courage

Sometimes the current of our circumstances carries us to a place we don't really want to be. We find ourselves serving gods we don't really want to serve. We long for change, but just how we break out of our present mold and chart a new beginning is the question. Change can be scary even when you want it. Here is where the true faith of a diva can be put to the test. How much are you willing to risk—or even sacrifice—in pursuit of the life you really want? (Read Joshua 2:1-21; 6:12-23.)

Behind the Veil

Rahab looked out over the vast terrain. They were out there. She knew it, and so did everyone else in the city. There had been an uneasiness building like a soundless rumble beneath them as everyone became aware the Israelites were gathering against them. Not knowing their strategy or when they would strike was unnerving. And though they tried to draw some comfort from the fact they were surrounded and fortified by a tremendous wall, from what they heard about this people and their fearsome God, who had given them tremendous victories over their enemies, they felt like sitting ducks—helpless and vulnerable.

A knock at the door interrupted Rahab's thoughts, and instantly a weariness filled her body. The resignation bled throughout her system and a worldly wariness filled her eyes as she opened the door. Perhaps she would tell whomever it was that she was closed for the night. She was so tired of this life. At first the money had afforded her the lifestyle she had so badly wanted, but now her love affair with independence and endless trinkets had ended. It was replaced by a survivor mentality that kept her from retching every time another man reached out to her, but it didn't keep her from being sick after he was gone. Between visits, she would ponder her fate and how to escape it. Perhaps she would eventually be able to do exactly that if the linens she wove became a viable revenue stream. She would be able to transition into a life she could be more proud of. Her family would certainly be pleased, but it would elate her most of all.

The urgency of the knock broke her thoughts, and she hurried to the door, wondering at her visitor's impatience. She was really not in the mood. She knew the moment she opened the door the men standing there were Israelites. Part of her felt relief, the other a new consternation. They were known to keep to themselves, and she knew her services would not be required. But what did they want? Merely lodging for the night it seemed. In that case, they were welcome. However once they had crossed her portal, she knew this was no ordinary visit. They were spies sent to spy out the land. Surely someone had seen them enter the city and make their way to her house, which sat on the wall. The authorities would be at her door at any moment given the present climate of fear.

She had barely hidden them beneath the flax she kept drying on the roof when another knock, more insistent than the first, sounded at her door. She adjusted herself and her expression before opening the door to look straight into the eyes of the king's guard. "We've been informed two men are in your home. They are spies. By the king's orders, you must release them to us." Just as calmly as they delivered their orders, she replied, "They are gone already. I did not know where they came from. They left at dusk just as the gates were about to close. You should still be able to catch them if you hurry." As she watched their hasty retreat, she decided this would be the last time she would be at some man's beck and call. Perhaps she was hiding the spies for a reason. Perhaps their God had heard her cry for deliverance from this life. Perhaps this was her chance at the freedom she longed for. At this point, she had nothing to lose.

In the darkness, she made her way to the roof hoping they had not yet fallen asleep. *Nothing beats a try but a failure,* she thought to herself. Looking into their inquisitive eyes that she noted were filled with kindness instead of the customary lust, she launched into her proposal. "Look, based on what I have heard of your God, I know He has already given you this city. No one has the courage to stand against you. I know that your God is the supreme God of the universe. I am willing to trade favors. Your escape for mine. Promise me you will spare me and my family in exchange for helping you." One hesitated, but in the end they both agreed to spare her on the condition that she hang a scarlet thread in her window. Also, her family members must remain in her home. They would not be able to account for anyone who was not within the confines of her house, and they would not be bound by their oath to her if she betrayed them. After they agreed to the terms, she lowered them out of her window, instructing them to hide in the hill country for three days before making their way back to their camp.

Afterward, she lay down, contemplating the gamble she had taken to secure a new future for herself. She breathed a silent prayer. "God of Israel, if You are really out there, please hear my prayer and deliver me."

In the days to come, panic in the city grew to epidemic proportions as it seemed the entire nation of Israel was upon them. Slowly and deliberately, they had made their way across the land and literally camped at their doorstep. Their strange behavior was even more unnerving to the citizens of Jericho. The soldiers lifted no weapons and sounded no battle cry. They simply walked around the city incessantly blowing rams' horns as their priest followed after with what someone in the city said was a box that contained their God. It was maddening. Day after day they marched wordlessly around the city. How long could this go on? By the seventh day, the townspeople were praying they would just attack and put them out of their misery. Fear of the unknown was more devastating than a full-on assault. Just as they were settling into the routine of the endless man march, they noticed something was different today. Their march did not end after their customary round, they continued again and again. Once, twice, three times... The tension mounted as the sound of their feet grew more ominous with each time around. They lost track of how many times around they had marched, when all of a sudden it seemed as if the heavens were filled with their shouting.

The people in town didn't know if they were quaking within or if the ground was actually shaking beneath their feet. Many passed out from fear as the shaking turned to rumbling and their beloved wall began to crumble. Literally, it fell before their eyes, and before they knew it, the army was upon them, climbing over the wreckage and making their way into the now unprotected city.

From her window, Rahab watched the army each day. She and her family barely spoke. All had not come immediately when she called, but with each passing day another fearful member came, casting aside their disapproval of her to embrace a greater hope of safety. She welcomed them all with full understanding. She had never tried to justify her lifestyle to them. She had merely done what she felt she had to do at the time. Now, hopefully, all of that was about to change. And so she waited. As the walls of the city came down, so did her personal walls. In the midst of the terror, she felt strangely, wonderfully free. As the two spies she recognized came with others to escort her and her family away to safety, she breathed another prayer. "Oh mighty God of Israel, thank You! Today I pray that You will be my God and I Your willing worshipper forever." Something in the way Salmon, one of the spies, looked at her now, across from the campfire, told her everything was going to be all right...

SHE COULD HAVE: Resigned herself to accept her life as is, becoming the walking dead, convinced there was no way out for her, remaining stuck or becoming completely paralyzed.

WHAT SEPARATES THE DIVAS FROM THE GIRLS: Raw determination and courage. A resounding decision to answer the call within that decrees she was created for something greater than where she presently lives. A resolve to be set apart for God's purposes and a willingness to separate herself from anything that hinders her from responding to His invitation.

LIFE LESSON: Whenever we decide to take a leap of faith, God is sure to catch us and deliver us to safe ground— if the intentions of our hearts are in harmony with His plan for us. This we will know and recognize by the burning urgency of the Spirit within us yearning for change.

> *Let us strip off every weight that slows us down, especially the sin that so easily hinders our progress. And let us run with endurance the race that God has set before us. We do this by keeping our eyes on Jesus, on whom our faith depends from start to finish* (Hebrews 12:1-2 NLT).

A Diva Not Only Seeks, but Climbs to Higher Ground

Discontent or discomfort should never be viewed as a negative emotion if it is urging you to make a change for the better. Maybe it is a friend urging you above a life of mediocrity and encouraging you to embrace the endless potential of God's perfect design for your life. I believe sometimes God is just waiting for our sigh of exasperation to introduce new possibilities into our spirits along with visions of the incredible life that awaits us if we would only press past where we presently stand. The grass can be greener on the other side if we are willing to tear down some walls to get there. No risk, no glory. Surely anything worth having is worth fighting for.

How can we free ourselves from our present routines and entrapments in order to get the life we really want? Rahab took some bold steps of faith to get what she wanted. She sets the standard and challenges us to up our diva status by following her example.

1. Locate yourself.

No one can move forward unless she assesses where she presently is. This calls for total honesty. You cannot chart a new path for your life if you are not willing to face where you are and what is not working. You can't change something if you don't know what you are supposed to change. Ask yourself the hard questions and be willing to answer them truthfully. Remember, this is about you becoming a better you.

If you need help with this one, ask your most honest friends for an evaluation of your situation and purpose not to be offended by anything they say. Take it for what it is worth and balance all comments in light of what you are looking for—the truth. Ask them to tell you what they think is impeding your progress in life. This may be a difficult exercise, but no one will give you this type of information unless you make it clear you really want to know. Then make your own assessment of how you see your life going: What you like. What you don't like. What you ultimately want to see happen in your life. What you would do differently if you could wave a magic wand....

Rahab knew her present lifestyle was leading her toward a dead end, and she decided she didn't want to go there. She didn't know how to escape from where she was so she worked on a transition plan. The bottom line was she knew what outcome she really wanted. She wanted to be out of Jericho, no longer given to prostitution. Because she was clear on her goal, she was able to recognize the opportunity for getting it when it surfaced. Most of us miss the opportunity to move forward because we are not clear on what we want to move forward to. You must be able to "see" it in order to have it. This is the first rule of exercising faith. It is the substance of things hoped for.... You must locate where you are, but you must also locate where you want to be. This is the beginning of the rest of your life.

2. Switch gods.

You must now recognize what you are serving that isn't serving you. Although you may be professing strong faith, you may not be able to discern the subtle deception of other things or people being more lord of your life than you know, including yourself. Again, honesty is required. What you submit yourself to rules you in the end. Any unsurrendered desire, habit, or emotion you harbor is holding you captive and keeping you from the freedom you need to experience the quality of life you long for.

Your god might be the wall you've built around your heart that keeps you from experiencing the love you so deeply yearn for. Or it might be your desire for material things that keeps you trapped in a career that certainly pays you but does not fulfill you. It might be the opinions of others that cause you to do things or live a life that is not really you. Only you know what you are serving—what drives you and consumes you. If it is not really serving you, fulfilling you, leading you to the life you really want, it's time to tear down that altar.

Rahab knew the gods she served weren't working. She felt more trapped than ever in her life. She saw a God at work in the Israelites' lives that was showing up big time. Rising up, slaying enemies, adding wealth to the Israelites, protecting them, providing for them, causing them to be feared by other nations. His reputation preceded them and paved the way for them to acquire the life they wanted. Rahab wanted what they had, and she was willing to discard her former gods to get it.

God must be in control for us to have control because He is the ultimate source of everything we are looking for. Whatever we can't live without controls us, and if anything other than God becomes our lifeblood, we are under the thumb of a harsh taskmaster. The desire or perceived need for money will fuel us to push ourselves so hard we eventually burn out. The search for love has led many to all the wrong places where they end up feeling more unloved than before. The paradox of seizing our desires, "making things happen," only to lose them can be maddening to many who despair over the lack of fulfillment in their lives. Only you know who or what your gods are—those silent robbers of your joy and peace. Tear down the altars and make yourself an offering to the only God who can deliver you out of all your troubles.

3. Commit yourself to change.

You decide the day and the hour your transformation will begin. It is up to you. Remember, we are in a partnership with God. He is not sitting in heaven waving magic wands, although He certainly delights in performing the supernatural in special cases to remind us of His power and glory. For the day-to-day experience, He has given us everything we need in order to live according to His divine plan and succeed in exercising godliness. As we submit our plans and desires to Him, He is faithful to assist us toward a better tomorrow.

Decide the outcome you want for your life and submit it to God in prayer. Wait before Him. Allow Him to give you an effective plan for moving forward. You will be amazed at how easily things will unfold once God has given His stamp of approval. In some cases, you may experience a bit of a tussle if God is trying to teach you something about prayer and spiritual warfare. But basically, if you do your homework, you should be able to proceed with the assurance that God is with you and behind you even if things don't fall into place as easily as you would like them to. If you keep moving forward, things will eventually line up.

Plan your work and work your plan. Write things down. Chart your course as well as your progress. The Bible encourages us to write the vision and make it plain so we can run with it. I have found in my life that whatever I write down eventually comes to pass. What is not written will never come to light. Establish your thoughts and set the spirit realm in motion by defining a clear-cut plan for yourself. Check your progress. Are you moving forward? What is working? What is not? What do you need to adjust in order to advance? Stay on course and make adjustments and additions to your plan when needed. The conclusion to this thought process is to have a plan. Remain flexible and open to any changes God might want to make or any unusual method He might want to utilize to bring the change to pass. Remember you are *partners*. You're in this thing together.

4. Take someone with you.

The best plans in the world will always be those that bless and profit others in addition to yourself. These are contagious plans that generate excitement and invite enthusiastic helpers. Everyone wants to be part of a worthy cause. Everyone wants to make a contribution that matters. As you plan changes in your life, consider how the changes you initiate will affect others. How can your circumstance be beneficial to those you love and those you want to help in the long run? Remember, nothing about your life is just about you. Someone else will always be affected. Therefore, ponder your choices carefully.

Rahab didn't think about just saving herself, even though

she desired a change with all her heart. She knew she could not enjoy her newfound life if she did not secure the same freedom for her family. She included their safety as part of the bargain she made with the spies. Her freedom brought freedom to others. Ours should too. Her desire to be a blessing, even under the greatest of stressful and unusual circumstances, got God's attention. Later, she would be blessed with favor—marrying one of the spies she helped escape, as well as becoming the mother of Boaz and the grandmother of David, king of Israel. How's that for an about-face in life? From disdain to being revered. From being an outcast to being a member of a glorious family— the family of God. If your plan for a better life only includes yourself, your plan is too small. Think again, my sister. Reach higher, dig deeper, and dream greater dreams.

Diva Confession

I will not allow my mind, the opinion of others, or my present circumstances to set limits or deter me from reaching the full potential of the life God has designed for me. Instead, I will embrace His vision for my life and partner with Him to plan, do, and ful-fill my purpose.

Diva Reflections

✳ What things would you like to change about your life right now? Why?

✳ How have those things been keeping you from living up to your full potential?

✳ What gods do you need to get rid of?

✳ What do you need to do in order to change your situation?

✳ Who else will be affected by the changes you make?

✳ How will these changes be positive and beneficial?

The Divine Bottom Line

The changes we want really begin within. As we grow and evolve, life and people either respond to our transformation or our stagnation. In the end, we have more power to choose the action, as well as the response, than we realize.

Choose Your Battles

Silently flexing muscles
within that gave the strength
to do nothing,
to say nothing,
leaving her opponent to fight alone,
she waited...
waited for the war to be over
realizing this was but one battle,
one that was worthy of missing,
reserving her ability to go
toe to toe
for another time...
another battle of greater import....
Praying within,
she lifted her eyes heavenward
toward her certain defense,
awaiting her marching orders.
Upon receiving none,
she rested in the knowledge
that abiding in the fortress
of the secret place
was defense enough
to overcome
the most fearsome foe.
So having done all,
she chose simply to stand....

How to Win the War

Whether in the workplace, or in your own personal space, at times it seems as if you have to fight to keep your footing. Life and people assault us. Thinkingly or unthinkingly, arrows are thrown, gauntlets are cast down, and challenges confront us in one way or another. Either mentally, physically, or spiritually, we battle for our place, our space, our peace of mind. Sometimes in the heat of it, a diva must remember to maintain her posture because losing it will guarantee her defeat.

Sometimes it's not what you say, it's what you don't say. It's not always what you do, it's what you don't do that can make the difference between victory and defeat. Someone will throw you a sucker punch out of nowhere, and you've got to roll with it. How do you win without losing your self-respect, your cool, even your Christian values? People say hurtful things and do even worse sometimes. It's easier to handle the offense when it comes from a stranger, but what do you do when it's from someone you love? Does submission mean becoming a doormat? Where is the balance? And finally, how does one find the courage to stand alone when it seems those in authority are exacting their own agenda to benefit themselves? At times we find ourselves in tight spots, and we have to know which move to make.

A diva must have her war strategies worked out ahead

of time. In order to stay ahead of the game, life must be lived offensively versus defensively. Remember, whenever you react out of fear or anger, you will make the wrong move, say the wrong thing, and ultimately blow your chances for reconciliation or restoration. A settled heart and a made-up mind on the key issues of life, grounded in the knowledge of who you are, can go a long way in the midst of drama and controversy.

The Diva Defense

*F*ear, jealousy, insecurity, and ignorance have to be four of the most unattractive attributes anyone can possess. All of them make people do and say stupid, hurtful things. Knowing this going into battle makes it a lot easier to dance between the arrows others may shoot at us from time to time without getting our feathers ruffled. Don't attack the fruit—look at the root and it will expose what the real deal is. A true diva never fights her opponent on the same level. She seeks higher ground to make her conquests. She drives in the stake of victory before moving on...still a lady...still very much a diva. (Read Numbers 12:1-16.)

Behind the Veil

Silently she listened to the rising voices of Miriam, Aaron, and her husband, Moses. She had seen it coming like a distant storm rolling in on the desert. It started with the glances that were always averted when she made eye contact. Then there were the "huddles" as she called them—the low rumbling conversations that would stop the moment she got in close proximity. She wondered how long it would take Miriam and Aaron to approach their brother Moses with their list of grievances, of which she was sure she was at the top.

She wondered if Moses had even noticed their reaction when he introduced her as his wife. Though they were polite, she had seen the glaze of resentment that quietly veiled their eyes. The tightness at the corners of their lips even though they were smiling. The constriction of the muscles around their necks. Oh yes, she had taken note of every subtle nuance of their body language. It amazed her that these people, who knew what it was like to be slaves themselves, could harbor any bit of prejudice. Yet she watched them take note of the darkness of her skin in comparison to their olive undertones, emphasizing the difference in the texture of their hair, and sizing her up in their mental calculation of whether she was "acceptable." She knew they were not pleased their brother had married an Ethiopian. Of course they would never say this out loud and incur his wrath, so they danced around the issue. However, the melody of their words did not cover their real heartbeat.

They had taken to complaining about everything except what really troubled them. All of a sudden they had a problem with Moses relaying messages from God. Even though they had long ago abdicated the task of talking to God to Moses, fearing being in His presence themselves, they now took issue with this. After all, why must he be the only one? Couldn't they hear from God for themselves? Who had crowned him god and king? But the question they didn't ask, at least in the presence of Moses was, would his wife now have more access to him than they did? Would he heed her counsel before listening to them? Yes, it was their unspoken fears that screamed the loudest. And so she held her tongue, pitying them instead of fearing them.

But now the showdown had finally occurred. Moses did not know how to respond to their initial outburst. And then to his relief, he found he didn't have to. The conversation had not only kindled the interest of anyone within hearing range, it had even gotten the attention of Yahweh, God Himself, and He was not amused. He summoned them to meet Him at the tabernacle of meeting. And there His anger burned against Aaron and Miriam. After chastising them vocally, He departed from the tabernacle leaving Miriam afflicted with leprosy, her skin as white as snow.

Aaron pleaded with Moses, and Moses pleaded with God, but God meant to prove His point. Miriam would remain leprous and shut out of the camp for seven days. Long enough hopefully for her to understand what it was like to be isolated and discriminated against because of the condition of her skin. The rest of the nation waited for Miriam before moving on. As they began their trek once more toward the Promised Land, they noticed Miriam's worship had changed. Now more beautiful than ever, it came from a gentler, more loving, and submitted spirit. And when Miriam looked at her taking her rightful place beside Moses as they moved forward, her eyes reflected gratefulness. "Thank you for not acknowledging my foolishness," they seemed to say, "thank you for not saying what you could have said." "It was nothing," her eyes replied. And indeed it really wasn't.

SHE COULD HAVE: Driven her husband, Moses, crazy complaining about her in-laws. She could have confronted Miriam and Aaron herself about being racist, or she could have bent over backward to try to win their acceptance. She could have submitted to feeling inferior, or worse yet, inflicted criticism on others around her to make herself feel better.

WHAT SEPARATES THE DIVAS FROM THE GIRLS: A graciousness that allows God to fight their battles, understanding that some enemies cannot be fought in the flesh and some wars are simply not theirs to fight.

LIFE LESSON: The use of strength or force against a weak enemy will only get you labeled a tyrant. However, grace will bring understanding, peace, and lasting victory because the heart is where most wars begin. An internal war is of greater magnitude than the one that rages externally and requires different weapons.

For we do not wrestle against flesh and blood, but against principalities, against powers, against the rulers of the darkness of this age, against spiritual hosts of wickedness in the heavenly places. Therefore take up the whole armor of God, that you may be able to withstand in the evil day, and having done all, to stand (Ephesians 6:12-13).

A Diva Knows How to Hold Her Peace

Well, talk about drama! You know you've done something when you get God riled up. What "haters" don't know is when they criticize and "dis" others, God takes their comments personally. After all, He created the one they are picking on! The children's rhyme, "sticks and stones may break my bones, but names will never hurt me," is only partially true. Insults and criticism sting, penetrate, and sometimes leave lasting scars. Not everyone is grounded enough to let vocal assaults bounce off them. To try and defend yourself against them seems to only induce quicksand-like results. You find yourself sinking in the mire of the negative comments, being overwhelmed by them. In the end, they can suck the life out of you if you let them. I am intrigued with the fact there is no discourse on the reaction of Moses' wife in this heated exchange between the siblings. She is loudly silent. I think her silence speaks volumes and gives us some clear-cut principles for dealing with offense.

1. Get down to the real nitty gritty.

Never be so ego-bound as to assume it's all about you. Most of the time, if you dig beneath the surface of the issue, you will discover it had little to do with you at all. Your part in the play is to unmask the true subtext of what is unfolding inside that person's heart—their own fears, insecurities, and petty jealousies. This is why you cannot afford to get excited. There is still too much information to gather.

What is *not* said is just as important as what is said in these situations. Aaron and Miriam complained because Moses married an Ethiopian woman, yet they went on a tangent about who got to talk to God. Somewhere in between these two points the real issue lies. Yes, they looked down on her, but the actual fear, while they were thinking themselves above her, was they really felt beneath her. All of a sudden there was another layer to wade through in order to get to Moses. Would she have more influence over him than them? What would that mean for all of them as they traveled to the Promised Land? It really wasn't about her after all. It was really about their own fears of being displaced and losing control. Again, never stop at the fruit—examine the root of the issue and there you will find the true source and cause of the battle.

2. Don't get mad, get sad for your offender.

How could you possibly get angry and harbor resentment against someone who has made themselves a prisoner of their fear and insecurity? When left to their own devices, these people usually self-destruct on their own. Time blows their cover and exposes them for what they truly are, and you walk off smelling like a rose.

The other frightful thing that happens when you stand back and hold your peace is God gets involved. This could make for a not-so-pretty picture depending on the offense. He has a special way of making your offenders get a true taste of empathy and relate to your pain by allowing them to experience what they made you experience. You couldn't design this one any better, so simply stay out of the way.

At the end of the day, between the offenders' painful internal issues that have them in a state of discomfort and the greater discomfort that comes from having to now experience the pain they've inflicted...well, it is not an enviable position, and one can most certainly spend better time praying for the offenders than being upset by them. They are in trouble. You are not.

3. Stay out of the fray.
Gracefully watch the battle from the sidelines, especially if there is a third party involved. There is never any need to defend yourself against someone else's problems. Remember, it really has little or nothing to do with you.

If you feel the need to ask your offenders questions, feel free to do so, only be clear on your motive. If you are trying to gain a better understanding of where they are coming from, and also help them to locate themselves in the instance (that is if they are even listening to themselves, most people don't when they are wound up about some-thing), then this might prove a profitable exercise. But if you are really trying to get them to see your side of the matter, this will probably not work out to your satisfaction. The reason being that most people feel completely justified in saying and doing what they've done. You cannot con-vince them otherwise. The Book of Proverbs states a fool is right in his own mind. There is no such thing as arguing with him, you simply sink to his level. When people are being offensive, they are being foolish.

In their foolishness, another dangerous thought pattern has set in. Literally, that person says in her heart there is no God without realizing it. She has chosen to be lord of the situation, removing God from His sovereign place in her life (if He was there at all), in order to "put you in your place." Ooh...step aside, sister, God will have none of that. God will not bow to any other gods or allow you to. That is when He arises on your behalf to do battle, to confront, correct, rebuke, and chasten if need be. Know who has your back, and let Him do the fighting for you.

You don't ever have to fight if you are right because God will fight for you. Your enemies are His enemies if you have claimed Him as your Lord and King. As your Abba Father, He does not take your affliction lightly. He has said that vengeance belongs to Him, and He will repay it. Now that covers two fronts. If restitution of any kind needs to be made, God will supply. He will also deal with your offenders. This completely disarms them and strips them of their power over you! There is no need to return to them, revisit the issue, or ask them for anything because God will take care of whatever you need. And that is the most liberating thing of all!

4. Forgive and move on.

In order to keep your liberty, you must be able to walk free of strife by forgiving and releasing the ones who hurt you and by moving on. To the measure you are able to forgive, God will forgive you. If you refuse to let go of the offense, you will find the tables turned, with you becoming the one in bondage. Therefore, it is as much about you as it is about them when it comes to letting go of the offense, as well as the offender.

Progress comes to a halt when we hold on to stuff that is better to let go of. In this instance, the entire nation of Israel had to wait for Miriam to be healed and return to camp before they could move on to the Promised Land! They were set back seven days because of this situation. Think of how your situation may be robbing you and others of the ability to move on if you refuse to let go of it.

"But I can't let go," some will say. The truth of the matter is, the only thing you can't afford to do is to hold on to it. That gives the other people way too much power. The best "revenge" you can exact is to do the opposite of what they would like you to do. Their mission will be accomplished if you allow their actions to affect you long-term. But to break free, move on, and crown it off by being able to be genuinely concerned for them and gracious about it? Well, that is a true diva move! One that separates you from the rest. One that definitely puts you ahead in the game of acquiring the promises and blessings of God.

Diva Confession

I will not allow myself to be bound by the criticisms and offenses of others. I will accept the grace God gives to me in those moments, allowing Him to be my defense. In light of this, I purpose to release my offenders and move on.

Diva Reflections

✳ What is your response when others criticize or offend you?

✳ What does your response garner?

✳ Does your reaction help or hurt the situation?

✳ What could you do differently in these types of situations?

✳ How long do you usually hold on to, nurse, and rehearse an offense?

✳ What would help you let go of it sooner?

✳ What concrete steps can you design for yourself to help you move on?

The Divine Bottom Line

When we feel the least powerful, there is always something greater at work—the grace of God. It is His power that places us out of harm's way and restores our hearts to a place of peace.

The Diva Position

Decisions, decisions. What to do when you are not the one in authority. How does one walk in submission to a boss, husband, or other figurehead during the times when his or her leadership is in question in your mind? You're a diva. You're smart, able to make things happen, and you can think of a better way to solve this problem...Ooo, anyone been in this position before? Well there comes a time when not yielding could cost you more in the end. So you take a deep breath and go along with doing things "his way." Are you still a diva? Most definitely, but now you've reached a new status—a diva refined. (Read Genesis 12:10-20; 20:1-17.)

Behind the Veil

Sarai took one last look at Abram before turning to follow the Pharaoh's guards into the palace. Why she had agreed to Abram's plan she would never know. Well, that wasn't exactly true. She had always trusted him, and he had never let her down before. She knew her husband heard from God, and she had to admit she was not always privy to those conversations. She didn't always understand some of the directions God gave to Abram, but in her mind, she had no choice. She chose to follow him. He was her husband and lord.

So when Abram approached her suggesting they introduce her to the Pharaoh as his sister, not his wife, it was the one time she was sorry she was so beautiful. What had been a source of pleasure to her husband now put them all at risk as they wandered through this strange land. She reluctantly agreed, comforting herself with the fact they weren't lying—exactly. She was his half sister—they shared the same father, but had different mothers, so it wasn't *really* a lie. But why couldn't Abram trust God to protect them from Pharaoh when he had had enough faith to uproot their entire household to go to a place God had not revealed yet? There were a thousand questions going through her mind, but she silenced the voices by gazing around at the finery of the palace until a new question burned into her core as she stood at the entrance of Pharaoh's harem. The Pharaoh's intentions were clear. What would happen should he decide to take her?

She squeezed her eyes shut as if to blot out the thought. No! If Abram couldn't trust God to keep them, she would have to exercise her own faith and dare to believe He was able to keep her from harm. Taking a deep breath she entered, leaving herself in God's care.

And then the plagues began. One after the other. It seemed every time the Pharaoh tried to be near her, a rash of disease broke out throughout the palace, ravaging everyone in the household—that is, with the exception of Sarai. Finally, the Pharaoh put two and two together. Summoning Abram, he fought to contain his fury, "Why didn't you tell me she was your wife and not your sister? Please take her and go!" And how they left! Pharaoh had been very generous to Abram, bestowing him with bountiful measures of livestock and servants. Still, Sarai said nothing, praying that her husband had learned an important lesson, and they could move on now that she was safely back in his presence.

Needless to say, once again, she could not believe her ears as he stood before the Philistine king Abimelech saying, "She is my sister." *Why, oh why, did it take men so long to learn?* she thought to herself as she said the words as if on automatic, "Yes, he is my brother." Once again she found herself the member of a harem, but the lush surroundings were lost on her as she wondered what God would do to deliver her this time.

The answer came quickly. Summoned before Abimelech, he told them of how God had revealed to him in a dream Sarai's true identity and threatened him with death should he touch her. Surrounded by his advisors, whose eyes were filled with fear, he returned Sarai to Abram, including an offering of a thousand shekels of silver to cover her trouble, along with all the livestock and servants he had already given him. He then told him he was free to dwell in the land wherever he liked; however, he did not appreciate his deceit. How could a prophet of God do such a thing? Would Abram please pray for his household's restoration? (The Lord had closed the womb of every woman in the court.)

As Abram prayed for the king and his household, Sarai also prayed, but her prayer was a different one. When Abram raised his head and gazed into her eyes, she saw the unspoken sentiment. "Never again, my wife." And she bowed her head and whispered, "May it be so."

SHE COULD HAVE: Given her husband Abram a lecture about the sin of lying or at least berated him and questioned his spirituality. Or worse yet, refused to do as he asked.

WHAT SEPARATES THE DIVAS FROM THE GIRLS: The understanding that their power lies in submission even when what they see doesn't make sense. They understand that when they are in the right position, God is able to move on their behalf.

LIFE LESSON: It is important to remember that our lives are not in the hands of any particular individual. Our lives are in the hands of God—and God alone. As we trust Him to cover and protect us, our only concern should be that of making sure we are in the right position to be kept. God will always honor an obedient heart. Every diva trusts her Savior to keep her safe and secure in His everlasting arms of love. Leaving the things she cannot control in the care of God is the surest way to experience lasting victory.

> *Wives, submit to your husbands as to the Lord....*
> *Now as the church submits to Christ, so also*
> *wives should submit to their husbands in every-*
> *thing* (Ephesians 5:22,24 NIV).

A Diva Lives Above the Power Struggle

Who can figure God out? As He says, His ways are truly not our ways. In His mind, the way up is down. The way to gain power is to release it. Pray for your enemies...It all seems a little backward doesn't it? However, it does work! A true diva does not waste time on the same lesson over and over. She learns to do what she can and leaves the rest to God. Whether she is in the position of serving a husband, employer, pastor, parent, or some other person in authority, the principle of submission must be mastered in order to experience victory in every situation and interaction.

Now for those of you who are admitted "control freaks," I know this sudden turn has your hair on fire, but bear with me. I've said it often: Submission is not about being a doormat, it is about putting yourself in the position to be blessed. I am by no means advocating you submit to an abusive situation—emotionally or physically. That is not God's will for anyone. I am addressing the day-to-day inter-actions at home as well as in the workplace, church, and community at-large. God holds those in authority over you responsible for your well-being (Hebrews 13:17). There-fore, it behooves them to lead you wisely. But what is your part in this whole order of God? And how can you stay in the right position when the directions you are being given are held in question in your mind? *Where is the balance in all of this?* I hear you screamin'.

I think our sister Sarai, later to be renamed Sarah, stuck to some principles in a difficult and questionable situation and came out shining like a true diva, as well as a lot richer for the experience.

1. Consider the source.
This is big. Who are you submitting to? Are these people who love you? Who have your best interest in mind? Would they deliberately

ask you to do something that would cause you
pain? Do you trust them enough to allow them
to make decisions concerning your life?

This is why husband selection is so important. God puts
that man in authority over you to lead you, protect you, and
provide for you. If you're too desperate to be married, you
can overlook major issues that reveal the character of the
man. Instead of taking note of integrity, sound character,
and wisdom, many opt for chemistry, good looks, and the
present romantic feeling. Ah, but the romance quickly ends
when they begin to disagree on the direction for their lives
as a couple.

On the flip side, that man is going to be blessed or
cursed based on his ability to lead you because God is
holding him accountable for your care. If you've taken over
leadership in the relationship, you have put that man in a
bad place with God. I'm sure Sarai balked within when
Abram proposed they identify themselves as sister and
brother on their travel route. I'm sure it didn't sit well with
her, yet she cooperated. Don't blame her submission on
biblical days because it is clear that she knew how to speak
her mind and get her way when she wanted to. After all,
she got Abram to send his son Ishmael away when she was
no longer amused with him or his mother Hagar! This
strong woman was also a woman who called her husband
"lord."

I believe Sarai considered the source and decided to
trust Abram, believing he had a good reason for this direction. But beyond trusting her husband, she trusted God
even more to protect and keep her if her husband's hunch

proved detrimental. This is important because the person in authority does not make the best decision in all cases. It is in these moments that we must be very sensitive spiritually, walking carefully and leaving room for God to move and set things in the right order. In yielding to the ones in authority without challenging their wisdom in the matter, you receive favor from God. This does not mean you shouldn't ask questions. Asking for clarification is vastly different from confronting them on their thought processes in a way that questions their leadership. Just know that even when you ask, sometimes you might not get an answer that will make you feel any better. It is in this moment, unless it is something life-threatening, that you must walk it out in faith.

2. Don't judge your circumstance in the natural.
More often than not, things are not what they seem. That includes our reasons why we do what we do. You think you are doing something for one purpose, yet you find out later that God had something completely different in mind.

Just when you think you have life figured out, God throws something else into the ring. He will not be limited by our plans or even our calculations on how to attain and acquire our desires. Here are Abram and Sarai, wandering through the land going to a place they are not sure of yet. As they stop along the way, God supernaturally supplies for them, adding wealth to them as they go. I'm sure Abram thought his time at Pharaoh's and King Abimelech's was about a stopover. He also probably thought their fascination with Sarai was all about her beauty, but it is clear that God used both of these circumstances to bless them not only with material wealth, but also allowed them to plant seed for their own miracle later in life. When Abram prayed for the wombs of the women in Abimelech's house, he opened the windows of heaven to also bless the womb of Sarai.

Stay open to the possibilities of God. Know that He is able to work the situation out for the good, no matter how shaky it may look initially. This is when God does His greatest work.

3. Wait long enough for God to act.

The temptation is always great when we can't see the road map clearly to take driving into our own hands. Where men stop asking for directions and just decide to keep driving, women want to stop, ask directions, and adjust the route. Sometimes God challenges us to walk by faith and not by sight.

The secrets of heaven are God's way of protecting our blessings until it is time for them to be delivered. If we truly trust Him, we will wait for Him to clarify the way we need to take in the light of His divine purpose and plan for our lives. He knows the plans He has for us, but we do not. All we can do is trust and wait on Him to reveal all things in His time. This calls for looking beyond the physical person in authority to remember God is ultimately in charge. It is really He who must resolve the situation you are in. The other person is simply the conduit for getting you to where you are. The director behind the scenes is still God. He is the One who ultimately calls "lights, camera, action." The scene plays out based on how you respond.

If you are walking in trust, God is able to honor that and come through for you. However, if you are operating in fear or doubt, trying to help God out by taking matters into your own hands, you might find yourself in more of a pickle than you anticipated. The reason for this would be you weren't privy to all the facts you needed to make your decision, leaving you to short-circuit your own blessing. But when we wait upon the Lord and ride it out, allowing the scene to unfold as it should, we get the bigger picture on what God is trying to accomplish. This is where faith partnership comes into play. When we throw up our hands and say, "I don't understand exactly why we have to take this route, but I will trust God and wait for Him to act. His timing is always perfect, and His heart toward me is a heart that is determined to unfold plans that are good and not evil, to give me an end He already planned before I arrived in this place."

4. Be willing to allow others to learn the lesson God is teaching you both.
Yes, I did say *both*. You better believe God doesn't waste anyone's time in the scheme of life when we find ourselves treading unfamiliar waters. Especially when you feel the most out of control...that is when God is working things out to the greatest good.

Not everyone gets the lesson immediately; therefore,

you might have to walk through some repeats. This is not the time to point fingers or scream, "Why are you not getting this?" No, it's time to look within and ask yourself, "What is God trying to teach me through this experience? How did I respond the first time? How can I deal with things in a better fashion this time around? What does God want to have happen in this situation?" This will keep you busy. Hopefully busy enough to keep you from railing at the other person, or trying to "teach" or "help" him or her get it right. In order to own the ball, the person in authority must catch it.

Learn your lessons and allow others to learn theirs. Recall a time when it took a while for God to get through to you. A time when it was hard for you to trust, wait, and see the profit in doing things the right way. Whatever it was, we've all been there. And still God was faithful. The secret to victorious submission is fully realizing one potent theme—God is ultimately in control. So it's not really about your husband, your father, your pastor, your boss, the president...*every* knee must bow to God in the end. The one you submit to must submit to a higher authority as well, to One who has everyone's good in mind.

Diva Confession

I will embrace the opportunity to walk in submission as a gift from God. A gift that brings me closer to the favor, blessings, and victory I desire for my life because God is not just my King, He is my Ultimate Source.

Diva Reflections

✳ What is the greatest thing you fear you will lose if you submit to those in leadership over you?

✳ What do you feel you control at present?

✳ What makes you most nervous when others take the reins?

✳ What would help you to let go and trust in these instances?

✳ Have you ever been in this situation before?

✳ What happened then?

✳ What did God prove to you in that instance?

✳ What did you gain from the experience?

✳ What lesson was learned?

✳ How can that be applied to your present circumstance?

The Divine Bottom Line

You will never gain more than you are willing to release. God will not pry open willful hands; however, He will graciously and lovingly deposit amazing gifts into open hands.

The Diva Principle

*T*here comes a time when you have to decide what you stand for and who you will stand behind. On that day, you will have to decide between your peers and standing on principle. On doing the right thing versus being popular. On preserving what is important in the face of intense opposition. Of perhaps surrendering your own power in order to yield to something greater. Of doing that one thing that fulfills your purpose. A move that affects kingdom living far beyond what you could imagine. (Read 2 Kings 11:1-16.)

Behind the Veil

Jehosheba crept along the corridor carefully, remaining out of sight. To be discovered now could cost much more than she was willing to pay. Her heart was heavy as she thought of the fact it had come to this—defying her own mother. Athaliah was on a murderous rampage. She was just like her mother, Jezebel, so hungry for power she had literally manipulated and controlled her son Ahaziah so she could run the kingdom. Now that he was dead, she was unwilling to give up the throne. In order to seize leadership completely, she decided to murder her grandsons so there would be no successors to the throne.

As news of the plan reached Jehosheba in the temple, she grieved over how misguided her stepmother was. She could not relate to this thirst for power. Rather, she rejoiced in the power of the Almighty God and chose to serve Him alongside her husband. She, a princess, had totally gone against the system by marrying a priest. And now she must go against part of her family again. She must preserve the life of her nephew, Joash, the rightful heir to the throne. If she could, she would save them all, but then she would risk discovery. Some would have to be sacrificed for the greater good. It was a matter of preserving not just one life, but an entire kingdom. She felt an urgency in her spirit to save him. She breathed a prayer for protection and went about her task.

Hurrying the infant away along with his nurse, she hid him in the temple. She knew that was the last place Athaliah would like him to be. After all, it was the last place she wanted to set foot in. And there Jehosheba held her peace, nurturing him and raising him in the fear of the Lord until the appointed day on his seventh birthday, when he would be installed into office and Athaliah and her wickedness would be done away with once and for all, hopefully along with the altars of Baal she had erected.

It was with a grateful heart that she watched Joash take his rightful place as king. All she, along with Jehoida, had taught him in the temple came to light as he honored the Lord throughout his reign. If she never did another thing, she knew it was for this reason she was created—to save and raise a king.

SHE COULD HAVE: Given into fear and resigned herself to suffering under the evil reign of Ahaziah. She could have decided it was more important to preserve her own life than that of the infant and allowed him to die.

WHAT SEPARATES THE DIVAS FROM THE GIRLS: The ability to see the big picture and place kingdom priorities above all else. Commitment to the greater good no matter what the cost.

LIFE LESSON: Going against the grain of your peers might appear to cost you everything but in the end, choosing the greater good bears lasting fruit that benefits count-less others. The sacrifice of one becomes a small price to pay in comparison.

> *As the branch cannot bear fruit of itself, unless it abides in the vine, neither can you unless you abide in Me* (John 15:4).

A Diva Affects Her Kingdom for the Good

In the struggle for power, many lose their integrity, reducing themselves to tactics that not only get them where they want to go, but also destroy others along the way. On the way up, no one who operates in this manner stops long enough to ponder the fact that those who rise to the top by force will always have to use force to maintain it. What you reap you will sow, no doubt about it. In the end, these people meet with a bitter end. How Jehosheba escaped all the palace intrigue and social climbing is beyond me. Instead, she opted for being the wife of a priest and living out her days serving God. Truly she was an instrument of

God at a crucial time in history—from the saving of a king to the preservation of a nation. I doubt if on that fateful day she even thought all of that through. No, I would dare say our dear sister just became infuriated about the treachery of Athaliah and decided enough was enough. She would not stand by and idly allow this woman to kill the next king.

Some of us are called to save kings, to go against peers who would further their own agenda regardless of what it costs others. A true diva cannot and will not watch from the sidelines. She is an active participant in her home, in her job, in her church, in her community. She stands against wrong and seeks to preserve peace. How she achieves it is not only an act of courage on her part, it's an act of grace. Jehosheba made some crucial decisions and stuck by them. The fruit of her efforts was evident in the kingdom for more than 40 years as the king she hid away, groomed, and raised for service worked to turn the nation back to God and to repair the temple. How can we fit into the kingdom agenda where we are? By following her example.

1. Call things what they really are.

Now is not the time to be politically correct. The more we do nothing, the more evil will prevail. It must be put in check. If you see the situation for what it is, then you have choices to make based on what you see. Denial, excuses, and being apathetic will not reverse the course of events. Only prudent action can save the day.

Realize that when things become clear to you in a situation, it is because God wants to work through you to bring about a solution. Depending on who is committing the wrongdoing, it can be difficult to look at the situation and call it for what it is. Jehosheba knew this little boy was supposed to be king. She could not stand by and see the purpose for his life get thwarted. We must be sensitive to God's purposes as we observe the dramas unfolding before us and be committed to the bigger picture and kingdom plan versus personal agendas.

Confronting loved ones or those close to you can be difficult and uncomfortable, but keep in mind you do more harm when you stand by and allow them to continue on their self-destructive path. This is called enabling. If you see it and don't call it, you become a participant. It's called standing on principle. Someone has to do it. Why not you? The bottom line is...if God allowed you to get wind of what was going on, He wants to use you to do something about it.

You can begin with prayer. Don't pray to have God elect someone else to deal with the situation, but pray to gain wisdom and strength to do what you must do to set the state of affairs right. In order to do this, you will have to make a clear assessment of what is going on before you decide the best solution. Now is not the time to fly off the hook and confront the person openly. This might aggravate the situation. Walk circumspectly—perhaps the solution is not an obvious one. This is why it is crucial not to simply react. Make a plan and quietly do your work, knowing God has your back.

As we come to the defense of others, God comes to our defense. We all are called to save a king or a queen of sorts at some point in our lives because we are all created to reign and rule over something. As we live and move in our mini kingdoms at home, work, church, and neighborhoods, we will be called to rise to the occasion and do something that affects others for good.

Although this can be applied to a broad principle, I would like to hone in on children for a moment. You never know the potential of a little one. Many mothers smother their children, killing their spirits, because their kids are the only things in their world they can control. I submit to you today that you have a little king or little queen in your midst that you have been given on loan from God. Your job is to prepare that young charge to reign and rule effectively in life. If you don't have a child, you have been called to do as Jehosheba did—to take a child under your wing (you may be saving him or her), nurturing character and wisdom in that developing soul. To prepare that child for the awesome task of fulfilling his or her God-given purpose. There is nothing like the joy of witnessing this child in later years walking as a responsible young man or woman, knowing you contributed in some way to who the person has become. This is a responsibility none of us can shirk.

2. Press past fear and personal limitations.

We can all have a million excuses for not taking action, but unfortunately none of them will cut it as long as God is on the throne as an empowering force. The list of excuses can be a long one. I'm not smart enough, good enough, strong enough, rich enough, educated enough....I'm just not enough; therefore, I can do nothing. Actually, that is a good place to start.

The faster you realize you are the vessel and not the source of the solution, the better off you will be. Now you can partner with God—really hear His voice and follow His directions to bring about a solution that is peaceable and effective. As recorded in the Bible, God constantly chose those who felt ill-equipped to perform some pretty daunting tasks. Challenge Pharaohs, slaughter enemies, kill giants—you name it, they did it. Not in their own power and wisdom, but as they were led by God. He deliberately chose those who did not believe their own press because He knew they would be dependent on Him for the solution to the problem they were addressing. He never sought out those who were full of themselves or power hungry because He knew their personal agendas would eventually override His kingdom agenda. Only the heart that is aware of its own shortcomings and insufficiencies can be a candidate for the high honor of partnering with God to effect change in the lives of others.

3. Take action.
Yes, you will be called to "do something." Jehosheba knew she could not stop Athaliah's rampage, so she quietly stole the child away and hid him. She then left the queen mother to those who had the strength to deal with her. God will not ask you to do anything you are not equipped to do. You may be called to be a place of sanctuary for someone who has been hurt and wounded or threatened emotionally,

physically, or spiritually. Don't look the other way. You are your brother's and sister's keeper.

Most of the time a simple solution can be applied to situations when we see people are not functioning in integrity and are wounding others or making power plays that are not conducive to the collective body at work. Sometimes it's gently asking the perpetrators about the motives for their behavior. If they have any character, as they locate themselves they will be convicted to make a change. On the other hand, they may feel they have the right to do what they are doing. Then perhaps the target of their behavior needs to be built up and nurtured in order to preserve that person's spirit and give him or her the strength to not cave in. In any case, you might not feel you are equipped to be a "hero" in the situation, but one sentence can make a difference. One act of kindness. Lifting a standard quietly. Remember, for every action, there is a reaction. Shining a light will always dispel darkness. Just make sure you do it in love and not in anger or indignation.

4. Complete your assignment.

Sometimes what you thought was a simple fix becomes a long-term assignment. Do the work. Be willing to go the distance with people. Don't treat them as projects. Be aware that God has chosen to use your life to affect and nurture someone else, preparing him or her for something significant that might or might not be revealed right away.

I have found in my own life the people who irritate me the most usually end up being people God has placed in my life for me to effect a change. As I submit to walking with them and loving them, they unfold like flowers and the most beautiful people emerge who then go on their way to do wonderful things for God.

Jehosheba was not called just to save a child from death; she was called to nurture him, raise him in the ways of the Lord for seven years, and prepare him for one day becoming a king. Her contribution to this little boy's life was felt throughout an entire kingdom. He was a king who was concerned about the spiritual climate of his country, and he took steps to call the people to order.

We must overcome the temptation to short-circuit the work God might be trying to do through us when we feel we've put in enough time on a person or situation. How long does it take? As long as it takes to complete what God has begun. Follow through. Decide to go the distance with that person. You will reap a reward in the end. The battle for people's souls rages around us on any given day. We must be willing to snatch people from the fire, as well as out of the line of fire, to save their souls and perhaps save many others through the life of one.

Diva Confession

I will not be an observer when I can be a participant in the plan of God. I will willingly partner with Him to touch, to heal, and to deliver others in order that they may effectively fulfill the purpose for which they were created.

Diva Reflections

❋ When others behave in an unseemly fashion, what is your reaction?

❋ What things stop you from being involved in situations that cause you concern?

❋ How do you handle conflict?

❋ Is there a better way to accomplish a peaceful resolution? What is it?

❋ How responsible do you feel for others?

❋ Are you able to see the gifts in the lives of others and encourage them to fulfill their purpose?

❋ In what ways do you do this?

❋ What is your motivation for nurturing others?

The Divine Bottom Line

Jesus came to save us all collectively, but now, by His Spirit, we are all called to save someone from the awful bondage of a life lived devoid of purpose or a thwarted destiny.

Keep the Faith

Moving mountains from where she stood,
    she focused beyond the horizon
        to the heavens
            where her help came from...
unmoving,
    unchanging
        in every circumstance,
            she chose to keep the faith.
    And for every time
    she reached the end of herself,
she revisited the well,
    drawing from a strength
        that was not her own,
    drinking it in...
allowing her
    to walk the extra mile
        to seize things beyond her reach,
            to obtain the invisible,
                to do the "impossible."
    And for every wall she encountered,
she spoke to herself
    "keep the faith."
        Opening her spiritual eyes,
            she looked beyond
        what she saw
            to see what
                He saw.
        Following where His finger pointed,
    she walked by faith
        and not by natural sight,
            looking past
                all the "buts,"
                    the "hows,"
                and the "whys,"

to the "now faith is,"
finding all she longed for
wrapped in neat little presents,
surrounded by her prayers
and His grace.
Now finally with her desires
laid to rest,
she sighed a contented sigh,
"So glad I chose
to keep the faith…"

How to Soar

Someone once said the difference between a successful person and the rest of the populace is one did something with the idea she had and the others didn't. Quiet as it's kept, what it really comes down to is faith. Someone took a chance while the others chose to play it safe. In order to break through the glass ceiling, whether it is self-imposed or put in place by others, we must learn to spread our wings and not just fly, but S.O.A.R. (Surmounting Obstacles And Reigning). That's the name of the game.

To settle for less than your dreams is to live a life of mediocrity. God created us and fashioned us to not just survive, but to thrive. To not just maintain, but to overcome. To not just bloom, but to flourish. All of these verbs require a noun to be present in our lives: Faith. Faith is the secret weapon of every diva. It beats in her heart and separates her from the pack. While others question, she believes in spite of what she sees, hears, feels, and even sometimes knows. She reaches beyond herself to the invisible realm of endless possibilities, understanding fully that her own resources are limited at best, but God's resources supply her with all she needs and beyond.

Stretching her hands toward heaven and her heart toward God's throne, she boldly makes her requests known to Him out of a spirit filled with gratitude, praise, and expectancy in His faithfulness. She makes a stand and does not move until she gets an answer.

Others wonder at her, for her life is filled with miracles and divine surprises that cannot be explained in natural terms. The evidence of where her faith lies is manifested in the fruit of her life and her overcoming nature. She is one who does not walk around the mountain. She does not change her course. By faith she marches forward, moving obstacles with her prayers and confessions, claiming the promises of God left and right. This is a woman who knows her "rights" in the Spirit. She will not be taken advantage of by the forces of darkness. She is nobody's victim. She is a victor wielding an invisible sword while brandishing the shield of faith. By faith she lives, by faith she moves, by faith and faith alone, she stands.

Divine Determination

*L*et's face it, we all have issues. The only problem is, if most of us got real, we would have to admit our issues have us. We are bound, paralyzed, and rendered downright helpless in far too many cases. We have said the words "that's just the way I am" so many times we actually believe them, and yet our true woman within is still screaming to get out. She will not be silenced. She is determined to be healthy, whole, and victorious. Let her out, ladies! The life you truly want to live awaits you. Truly you are ready. If you have come this far, why stop now? Take a deep breath and know you are not alone in the struggle to get past your issues. One diva has proven it's possible and leaves the legacy of an example we can all live by. (Read Luke 8:43-48.)

Behind the Veil

She took a deep breath and moved forward, breaking past the invisible hands that had held her back for so long. She twisted now as if playing out the very act of wrenching herself from them. No! She was sick and tired of being sick and tired. Today was the day for something different to happen. Call it what you want—desperation, determination...

whatever—all she knew was that it was time for her change to come.

Clutching her garments around her, she could feel the constant trickle she should have grown used to after all these years but refused to. The words of an endless stream of physicians echoed in her head, "There's nothing I can do…" "Have you tried this?" "Have you tried that?" "I don't know what to say, perhaps it's something you're doing. Have you told me everything?" She shook her head as if to dismiss their remarks. Remarks that had hurt her more than her condition in some instances. Things said with attitudes that ranged from professional coldness, to bored apathy, to actually accusing her of being the cause of her condition.

Her friends had long grown bored with her dilemma, acting as if it were some shortcoming on her part that had brought this malady upon her. Some suggested it was all her fault she had not gotten past this. But it was when they began avoiding her like the plague, as if her condition would rub off on them or tarnish them in some way, that a new kind of pain settled in to seize her and make her feel more alone than ever. According to the law, for as long as the flow of a woman's menstruation lasted, she was unclean. Anyone who sat where she sat was also considered unclean and would have to go through ceremonial cleansing. Intellectually, she understood why they stopped visiting. Being her friend was just too much work, but the pain was still fresh and real after all these years. She couldn't help it! Didn't they understand? She would not be selfish if the shoe were on the other foot.

But none of that mattered anymore. Not her feelings about how her relatives and friends had grown weary of her suffering, as if they were the ones who had to live with it noon and night, day after day, month after month, year after year. Not the opinions of the doctors who gladly took her money, yet had no patience for her condition. She wanted her life back, and she would do whatever she had to do to get it.

With that resolve burning in her heart, she plunged into the crowd. The crowd that she should be nowhere near. Let them worry about cleansing themselves. She had been considered unclean for so long she was no longer able to separate herself from the label. All she knew was that she had to get to Him—this man they called the Messiah. The One who had been healing people as if it were second nature to do so. His reputation had preceded Him, and now the people thronged around Him, vying for His attention.

She could feel her strength slowly ebbing away as she struggled to make her way to where He was. Drained, she purposed to keep moving. *If I can just touch the hem of His garment, I'll be healed. I just know I will. No need to disturb Him, and besides, I don't need a conversation, I need results.* Feeling faint, caught between the heat of bustling humanity and her own physical lack of fortitude, she found herself crouching forward. Practically crawling, she fell to her knees, almost getting trampled by the surging crowd as she laid hold of the hem of His robe. How low would she go? As low as she needed to in order to get what she wanted. As her fingers brushed the well-traveled linen before it was swept away from her grasp, she was struck by an odd feeling. A sudden coolness ran throughout her body. It was as if time stood still. The constant trickle had ceased. Strength coursed through her body!

Slowly she stood to her feet. Taking in the feeling, and yet marveling at how foreign it all felt. The crowd continued forward, brushing past her impatiently as if she was impeding their progress. Then suddenly everyone stopped. "Who touched me?" He asked. His disciples all looked at Him askance. "What do you mean who touched You? *Everybody* is touching You. Look at the crowd!" "No," He insisted. "Someone touched me on purpose. I felt power leave me." And then His eyes met hers.

She moved forward trembling, whether from the fear of discovery or the joy of finally being made whole, she did not know. All she knew was she was healed and not going back to where she had been. "It was me," she heard herself saying through her tears. "Blood has not stopped flowing in my body for 12 years, and I have spent all I had seeking a cure with no results until today. Forgive me for breaking the law, but something told me that if I could just touch You I would be all right. And now I stand before You healed!" She held her breath waiting for His reply, not sure if He would rebuke her. Then she saw the kindness in His eyes. The light. The unbelievable grace and love she had never known. "Be of good cheer, daughter," He said, "your faith has made you whole."

"Your faith has made you whole." *My faith? No, the credit belongs to Him,* she thought. "Your faith has made you whole." The words echoed in her heart as she turned to go home. *The first thing I'm going to do when I get there is give my house a well-needed cleaning.*

SHE COULD HAVE: Accepted her fate in life and learned to live with her "issue." She could have built a life around her issue, milking it for all it was worth, and put things in place to accommodate her circumstances.

WHAT SEPARATES THE DIVAS FROM THE GIRLS: The refusal to bow to anything less than the will of God for their lives. The determination to reach beyond where they presently live and claim the wholeness that is rightfully theirs by faith.

LIFE LESSON: The only thing that separates us from the life we want to live is our own determination of the possibilities and the actions we are willing to take.

Let Your lovingkindness and Your truth continually preserve me (Psalm 40:11).

A Diva Gets Past Her Issues

There are so many things we've all lived with for so long that they threaten to become our "normal." After a while, we can actually be fooled into believing that's just the way things are supposed to be. Anyone who disagrees with this gets filed in the "they just don't understand" category. As we continue our solitary struggles, we secretly wonder if anything else is truly possible: Will I ever be whole? Have the love I long for? Fulfill my long-awaited dream? Be free from pain? Fear? Lack? Disappointment?

We've made a joke out of the phrase "Girl, you've got issues!" Ah, but it's really not funny. Issues become old news quickly, giving way to rancid sentiments of bitterness, resentment, and apathy. Not exactly what God wants us to experience. He has another realm of living in mind for all of us. How do we get past our problems and out of our present mold? I think a sister who is well-acquainted with issues, one in this context, can shed some light on the subject.

1. Dare to believe you have a choice, and go after what you want.

Your grasp on life will only go as far as the goals you set. Your goals should never be determined by your present circumstance. It is only by thinking outside the box that you move beyond your immediate boundaries. Therefore, explore and exploit every option available.

What do you want to see happen in your life? You must decide—and don't take no for an answer. We have been given the awesome power that is an extension of our heavenly Father's character. It is called the power to create. When God is in agreement with us, we become co-conspirators in birthing the desire He has placed in our hearts—to speak it, will it, and witness it manifesting. You must clarify your vision before you can run toward it. Otherwise, how will you know what direction to go in? Or even know that you should be moving? When Jesus approached the man at the pool of Bethesda who had been paralyzed for 38 years and asked him, "Do you want to be whole?" He was not being facetious. He wanted the man to decide what he wanted. If he were content to continue lying there, even if Jesus had dropped healing into his lap, he would not have gotten up because he would have no motivation to do so.

It is time to dare to make a decision about what you

want in life, no matter how foreign, ridiculous, or unbelievable it may sound. It is time to create a new "normal" for
yourself. It is not normal in God's eyes for you to be unful-
filled, to be anything less than whole. It should be "normal"
to you to see your desires becoming reality because you
walk in the supernatural. You see the invisible, you feel the
intangible, and you hear the inaudible. These things should
become second nature to you because you walk to the beat
of a different drummer. Your life is in tune with heaven's
rhythm. You will never be able to settle for the status quo.
You will always want more because God is calling you to
live by a higher standard, and you are answering the voice
you hear within. Set the bar, and then leap over it.

2. Talk to yourself.

If negativity is all you've been hearing, you
must drown out the external voices yourself.
Replace every confession that is not conducive
to you reaching your destination with something positive. No one will have the grace to
endure your situation but you. Others will not
because it is not their burden; they've got issues
of their own. In the end, there will be just you
and God, working it out together. If progress is
to be made, you must be in agreement with the
only One who can be an effective partner.

God will never agree with "I can't," "I'll never," or "It's
impossible." These words are not in His vocabulary. In this
case, whose report will you believe? The doctor or God?
Your friends or God? Your family or God? The media or
God? Statistics or God? Whose voice is ringing the loudest

in your head? If the voice is citing impossibilities, drown it out with the possibilities.

You might be saying, "Get realistic, Michelle." Sister, that's exactly what I am doing! God has fashioned our brain to be an amazingly complex and creative instrument. It cannot separate imagination from reality. It signals the rest of your body to line up with whatever it perceives as reality. If sickness is your mental reality, it will be your physical reality. If a life devoid of the love you want is your mental reality, the brain will help you sabotage every relationship to make it a physical reality. Are you getting this? Our diva with "the issue" decided not to listen to the doctors who told her she could not be cured. She made her way to Jesus, who became the last realistic choice she had left. In her mind, it was touch Him or bust. She went for it, and He told her it was her faith that made her whole. Her body lined up with the faith that a touch from Jesus would make healing a reality in her body, and it was so. Change your conversation! Tell your spirit what your new reality is, and command it to line up under the authority of what you believe. Then dare to take a faith walk.

3. Press past convention.

Truly we bind ourselves by our own rules. We follow them religiously and then wonder why nothing in our lives changes. In order to get different results, we must take different actions. Press past the "I can't do thats" to the "Oh, yes I cans, and I wills." Where there is a will, there is a way, I believe the phrase goes, and it is entirely scriptural. God was convinced, as recorded in Genesis 11:16, that if the people could determine what they wanted and agree to work together, nothing would be impossible to them. The same applies to you.

Friends and loved ones, as well-intended as they may be, can be your biggest hindrance at times. Out of fear and concern for you, they may caution you above and beyond what is true or necessary. For the most part, people are fearful of taking a risk even if they have no choice. Thus our fascination for TV shows like *The Amazing Race* and *Fear Factor,* where we live vicariously through others who are brave enough to seek adventure. It costs us nothing to watch, but the hidden reality is we would gain more if we could participate. Stepping outside of the box, choosing unconventional paths, "walking on the wild side" so to speak, is the way to freedom and wholeness.

There is nothing orthodox or conventional about God. He is outrageous! Parting seas, healing men in dirty water, spitting on people's eyes....I would dare say at times He used shock tactics to shake people up enough to remove them from the situations they had become so deeply entrenched in. They had to be caught off-guard so they couldn't argue with their deliverance. Before they knew it, they were walking, talking, and whole.

Our diva with "the issue" was not supposed to be in the center of a crowd, sullying everyone around her. (If we're honest, that's what most people are afraid of, that our stuff will rub off on them.) She was to remain on the outskirts of town, on the fringes of life, inside her own private hell called home, alone and isolated to deal with her issue by herself. But no... One day she decides to break out of everyone else's rules for her life and take matters into her own hands. She had run out of money, so she didn't have to worry about what her actions would cost her. She had nothing left to lose but her hope. She pressed past the boundaries that had been set for her, past her own fears, and focused on her outcome. Gathering momentum, she moved forward and took hold of what she wanted.

She distinguished herself from the rest of the crowd around Jesus, who was jostling against Him, by touching Him deliberately. She knew what she wanted when she touched Him, and she got it. She wasn't taking a stab in the dark, touching Him just to say she had touched Him. No... purposefully she reached out and her desire met with her faith in that instant, at the point of contact, with the One who had the power to right her situation—and the rest is history.

Determine what unrealistic rules are hindering you from receiving what you desire and abolish them once and for all. Dare to do something you haven't done before. Dare to embrace the results.

4. Claim your victory.

Sometimes we're afraid to vocalize changes because we fear them not being permanent. Tell the truth and shame the devil, I say. What you speak will be established. We as believers overcome by two things. The first is the blood of the Lamb—the price Christ paid for us to wipe out our sins and reestablish our relationship with God. The second is the word of our testimony. What we say happens in our lives because of Him who died for us. We have been given the authority to speak things into existence.

When questioned on the change in your countenance, you need to have a victory statement prepared. Whenever doubt tries to assault you and rob you of your breakthrough, you need to speak it out. *Oh no, I'm not going back there because on such and such a day, this thing happened that set me free from that!* You are going to have to put yourself in remembrance of your deliverance. No one is going to do it for you, especially if part of your crew is still bound themselves. You know that misery loves company; therefore, don't expect the bound to encourage you in your liberty.

Write and post your confession somewhere that is easily accessible for you to see all the time until it gets past your head and into your spirit, until it becomes part of you. Find a scripture to back up your confession so you can have the confidence that God is in agreement with you. He will help you maintain your victory. Know that you are surrounded by a great cloud of witnesses who have overcome every setback imaginable. Stand up and be counted, my sister. Truly you are not the only one with issues, and there is no issue you cannot get past. It is up to you when and how you overcome.

Diva Confession

I refuse to be bound by hindering thoughts and habits that keep me from being all I was created to be. I will arise and claim what is mine for the asking from God now.

Diva Reflections

✳ What is your recurring issue?

✳ What has become your "normal" in this situation?

✳ What would you like your outcome to be?

✳ What must you do differently in order for that to become a reality?

✳ What statements have been made by those around you that keep you bound?

✳ What new confession must you rehearse?

✳ How will you maintain your victory?

The Divine Bottom Line

What you settle for is what you will receive. The spirit who is able to envision a victorious outcome will chart its own course, defying the odds and arriving at its desired destination.

Divine Patience

*T*here are things in life that take their sweet time coming to pass. You've got to decide you are going to hold out for the gold. Sure, there will be appetizers along the way that can distract you from the main course, but you've got to stay focused. Either you trust God or you don't. Secret desires harbored in your heart that only He is privy to are not overlooked on His divine watch. But within His plan to give only good and perfect gifts, timing is crucial. The part that goes unrevealed to us until much later in the game is the foundation for our desires.

Most of the time we only see one aspect of what burns in our heart, while God sees the bigger picture and all the other people who will be affected by that *one thing* that seems significant to only you. Then one day, just as you have decided to release it, finally weary of clinging too tightly, it comes to pass and you are overwhelmed with gratitude and understanding of the greater plan as you witness the answer to your prayers. (Read Luke 2:36-38.)

Behind the Veil

Anna rose slowly from her knees, having completed her time of fasting and prayer. Her face was aglow, covered with the dew of joyful tears. She always wept when she felt the presence of God this strongly. He had never failed to meet her during her times of prayer and worship. For 84 years they had met here in the temple where she waited before Him. Eighty-four joyous years. She had thought her joy could never be restored after the death of her husband of only seven years. She recalled wondering how she would survive with no one to take care of her. And then she took to heart the words of Isaiah being taught in the temple that God would be a husband to the husbandless, that the barren woman would have more children than she who had a husband. These words rang in her heart, and she chose to see her time with her husband through different eyes. Seven years of preparation. The number of completion. Those years had taught her how to love and serve unconditionally, training her for her service to God. From the time of this revelation, she never left the temple. Continuing in fasting and prayer both night and day, she sought God's heart and shared what He told her with others.

And now today, as she made her way down the corridor to the main portion of the temple, she felt something different in her spirit. Today was not just any day. She could feel an unexplainable anticipation of some great occurrence. Just what it was she did not know, but she recognized the feeling. God was up to something, and it would simply be a matter of time before she found out what. All of a sudden, she did not feel as if she were more than 100 years old. It was as if her youth had been renewed. There was a lightness in her step as she picked up her pace, hurrying toward what she did not know. All she knew was she did not want to miss whatever it was that was about to occur.

She felt them before she saw them. The couple and their extraordinary baby. Drawing closer, she overheard the words of Simeon, another worshipper who spent many of his days in the temple, "Lord, now You are letting Your servant depart in peace, according to Your word; For my eyes have seen Your salvation which You have prepared before the face of all peoples, a light to bring revelation to the Gentiles, and the glory of Your people Israel" (Luke 2:29-32). Anna felt her heart leap as she surveyed the faces of the parents who seemed transfixed by Simeon's words, "Behold, this Child is destined for the fall and rising of many in Israel, and for a sign which will be spoken against (yes, a sword will pierce your own soul also), that the thoughts of many hearts may be revealed" (Luke 2:34-35).

Could it be? Anna thought, and the moment she saw the child's face she knew. This was the Messiah she had prayed for for so long. She clasped her hands to her heart overwhelmed with emotion. And then she could no longer stifle her praise. God had once again proven Himself faithful. He had not allowed her to die without seeing the promise made manifest. He had never failed or forsaken her, and now He had fulfilled His promise to redeem all of mankind. And she, Anna, a lowly widow, had been allowed the privilege of beholding this miracle of all miracles. As she went on her way proclaiming the good news to all who would listen, she felt her mission had finally been accomplished.

SHE COULD HAVE: Spent her days in bitterness and depression, bemoaning her hard luck and blaming God for robbing her of a life filled with love and family. She could have tried to remarry or make some other life for herself in order to fulfill her own needs.

WHAT SEPARATES THE DIVAS FROM THE GIRLS: The capacity to carry on in spite of tremendous loss and disappointment. The ability to channel pain into positive and productive avenues of service that effect lasting change in the lives of many.

LIFE LESSON: For everything we lose in this life, we gain eternal treasures that will manifest in our lives here on earth and extend to the life beyond. It is these precious gifts from the Father that become our greatest blessing, bringing unexpected joy and fulfillment to us and countless others.

> *Now faith is the substance of things hoped for,*
> *the evidence of things not seen* (Hebrews 11:1).

The Secret Life of a Diva

The greatest power a person may have is that which is unseen. If anything separates the movers and shakers from the ordinary citizens of the kingdom, it is the ability to gain access to the throne room of grace, the privilege to have audience with God and have Him respond to the cry of your heart. Prayer is the most intense, most intimate, and most dynamic tool any woman can experience and possess in her personal arsenal.

The question has been raised, How long does one wait on God? The answer: As long as it takes. His divine timing takes more into account than our desire for the answer. So we wait, in spite of the ticking of the clock—whether it be biological or external. We learn to wait on Him through the losses, through the trials, through the tears, and through the questions. And, like Anna, hopefully we learn a few things along the way that teach us to wait in a joyous state of trust and expectation.

1. Cash in your losses.

"Why me?" Famous last words that deserve only one answer, "Why not you?" We gain, we lose. This is the cycle of life. One should not take it so personally. Or perhaps you should. Perhaps God knew you were such a woman of substance He could trust you to handle loss gracefully and be an example to others of His amazing faithfulness.

Perhaps the pain you experienced, no matter how brief, was a divine setup for a heavenly promotion. In my own life, it was the death of my boyfriend that led me to Christ. What I lost was tremendous, but what I gained was even more amazing. The excruciating pain I experienced was replaced by joy unspeakable. My sorrow was replaced by a life I never expected to live, which has brought me to this place—of meeting you here on these pages.

All of this ministry was borne out of my own personal loss for the benefit of God's gain to address countless women held close to His heart. And His gain is always our gain. Was my first inclination to curl up in the fetal position and never recover? Of course it was, but then the devil would have won. He would have succeeded at ruining my life. Defeat is just not something in my vocabulary, so I decided to cash in my losses and get something out of them. The first realization you must have is that loss is never about just you. It is about something that God wants to do in your life to benefit yourself and others. Sometimes He has to make room for what He is about to do. His bottom line is always working things out to the good. He is a God of redemption. You can always cash in your coupons and get something good back. The choice is up to you. Hold on to your pain and lose even more than you planned, or hold up your empty hands to God and allow Him to fill them with more pleasure than you ever anticipated.

2. Redirect your focus.

Know that every void in your life must be filled with something; therefore, choose carefully. Whatever has been lost must be replaced. God wants to exchange good things with us. As we look to Him for our heart's redemption, He comes bearing gifts above what we could imagine, surprising us with joy. However, we must give Him a fair audience in order for this to happen.

When Anna lost her husband after only seven years of marriage, she was still a young woman who could have remarried, yet she chose to devote herself to serving God. Perhaps she initially went to Him seeking a balm for her pain and found more pleasure than she thought was possible. The fulfillment she got from spending her days and nights in fasting and prayer is evident in her disposition after spending 84 years in the temple. The joy, the enthusiasm she had came from living a life that she chose and from being rewarded for making the right choice. She determined to get past her own personal longings and invest her life into something that would benefit others beside herself.

Looking past her own pain, she chose to intercede for others. I'm sure she came to the conclusion that countless others had problems more severe than her own. This realization nurtured a grateful spirit that transformed her into a true worshipper of God. To be thankful for the moments of joy, and to be able to release them when they are over, is a gift within itself, and one that can take a lifetime to master. Pain can actually be a friend to us because it reveals how self-involved we are. The more we concentrate on ourselves, the more discontent and pain we feel. Consider it a bumper to thrust you back into the world of giving and loving beyond yourself. A place with more rewards than you could ever reap alone.

3. Give unconditionally just for the joy of it.
Service or waiting on God is a place of privilege few take advantage of because they fail to see what is in it for them. We want what we want. If we have no guarantee that God is going to give us our desires, we tend to go in search of securing what we want for ourselves. In the back of our minds, we rationalize that once we've gotten our business settled, we will then be free to give ourselves totally to God without being distracted by our lack. The words "those who seek to save their lives will

lose them, but those who seek to lose their lives will find them" are faint echoes in the back of our spirits, lost in the midst of our self-focused quest.

However, those who heed those wise words find the true power and joy of living. No longer serving God with any conditions other than the pleasure of serving ironically delivers all we've been searching for in the first place! In our mad dash for significance and love, we overlook the way to achieve both—by growing and contributing the fruit of our growth to the world. Getting over ourselves and going into the needs of others will always be more satisfying than examining our own belly buttons. Finding and hearing the heart of God brings a richness to life that is unparalleled. To feel as if we are part of something big, helping God birth His vision for healing and transforming others, brings a sense of fulfillment that cannot be described.

Sure, we all still have personal needs that don't go away, but there is a trust that enters the equation that settles the issues of the heart and gives us the grace to wait on God's perfect timing. To be lost in service can actually distract us from our needs. Service to things that matter reminds us to put everything into perspective. If every good and perfect gift comes from God, then when it is good for us, and a perfect fit for our lives and all concerned, God will deliver the desires of our hearts. It won't be a day too late or too soon. The truth of the matter is the nature of what we pray for dictates when some things we desire occur. Some may never see some of their prayers answered because the answer may not be completed until they've gone on. However, what our eyes see is not complete enough a picture to mandate how we testify to the faithfulness of God. He will finish everything He begins with or without our participation. The true satisfaction comes from knowing that our service and prayers are part of something so much bigger than us, and our present dreams and the results of our contributions are lasting.

4. Surrender.

Here is where a true diva's power really lies—when she can get to the point of living, loving, and serving unconditionally, not based on what she gets back. The freedom to live and love regardless of anyone's response is exhilarating. This is the place where God wants us to live and reign.

To be able to say, "If this never comes to pass in my life, I will still live joyfully and love God with all my heart," unlocks reservoirs of strength and liberation that enable you to live the life of your dreams unfettered by conditions. Most of us make life harder for ourselves than we need to—all because of the list of qualifiers we've decreed must be in place in order for us to be happy. Get rid of the list! If you don't, the list will control you. Jesus said He came that we might have life more abundantly, but in most cases, life has us. It should be the other way around, but we've bound ourselves up with our own rules. Surrender. Give God the option to do more than you would have chosen for yourself.

Surrender to the moment. Most of us are not present in the day-to-day because we're always worried about tomorrow, or which pasture is greener, or our list of "if onlys." But to live in the moment, affirming this is where God has placed us *on* purpose *for* a specific reason, helps us live life to the fullest every minute of every hour.

Surrender is not about giving up and becoming a victim of the life you feel is holding you hostage. Surrender is what you determine. It can be a place of reveling in the present—tasting and seeing that God is good right now and so is life. Actually, it's better than you thought it could be. Take advantage of the moment. Tomorrow will come quickly enough with its own problems and baggage. I've learned in my down times, when nothing is going on, not to worry about the inactivity. Things will get hectic soon enough. Instead, I choose to thoroughly enjoy the silence, the absence of the urgent, taking the time to rest and regroup. Surrender is by no means a passive act. It means you actively choose to let go of everything you can't do anything about. To grapple with issues beyond your control is to fight with the wind. You'll have nothing to show for all of the energy you expend. Truly surrender.

Surrender like the eagle that chooses to soar on the current of the wind. Initially he uses his wing power to gain altitude, but then he surrenders to the power of a force greater than himself, allowing it to carry him to his destination. Now that is faith! Faith helps you surrender because it knows you can never give something to God and not get something greater back. Faith also knows that the beauty of surrender is it releases the power to God to place you above some things and out of harm's way. It also lifts you to a place where you can gain a clearer perspective on life as a whole. And finally, faith gives you the power to surrender your timetable to God because it knows God's timing is perfect, and it is never too late for a blessing.

Diva Confession

I will seek the center of God's will for my life, keeping in mind that all of my experiences, including my losses, have equipped me to be a special source of blessing to someone with a specific need I have now been empowered to address.

Diva Reflections

✳ What is your attitude toward loss in your life?

✳ What is your response to occurrences that are beyond your control?

✳ What happens to your prayer life in the midst of upsetting circumstances?

✳ How can these times deepen your relationship with God?

✳ What can you focus on in times like these?

✳ Who can you reach out to serve?

✷ What conditions or qualifiers do you need to discard in order to make it easier for you to be joyful and fulfilled?

✷ What things do you need to surrender?

The Divine Bottom Line

It is not what we receive but what we pour our lives into that will last. The legacy of answered prayers and changed lives are the timeless contribution we leave behind as an example to others of what is truly important in the end.

Divine Trust

There is a place called "the end of ourselves" that is frightening and excruciating in its uncertainty and character altering. This place will make or break us. It is the place where we make the awesome discovery that can either fill us with greater fear or overwhelming relief that we are not in control of anything. We will either waste energy as we wrestle with our circumstances or we can rest in this place and allow God to do what He does best—come to our rescue in His usual spectacular fashion. The greatest hindrance to resting is us. This could explain why God has to allow us to bottom out—at times lose everything—in order to recalibrate our spirits and place things back in divine order. Trusting more in Him than in ourselves, more in Him than our hoarded resources, more in Him than in the strength and brilliance of people… Every diva must have a major moment of epiphany where she has to finally decide either "I believe God with all my heart" or "I don't." (Read 1 Kings 17:9; 2 Kings 4:2-7.)

Behind the Veil

Standing before Elisha, she weighed her words, being careful not to sound indignant, although that was exactly how she felt. Who her indignation was directed toward was hard for her to discern. Perhaps she really didn't want to face the fact she was upset with God. That sounded so ungrateful, so spiritually incorrect, and yet she could not reconcile her emotions to feel otherwise. After all, her husband had been a loyal servant to this mighty prophet of God, literally sacrificing everything to follow and serve him. He had placed God's business before his own personal agenda, and it seemed in the end to have cost them dearly. Now he was dead, and she was penniless with creditors knocking at her door, ready to take her sons away and press them into slavery in order to exact what she owed from them. It wasn't fair. This was not how serving God was supposed to pan out. What happened to Jehovah-jireh, the great provider? Where was He? How could one who had been faithful to God end up in this position? She bit the bottom of her lip to keep the words that pressed against the back of her teeth from spilling out in an embarrassing barrage. She would simply stick to the facts, how she felt about it would not profit her at this time.

And so she told Elisha her problem, to which he replied, "What would you have me do?" *What kind of question is that?* she wondered. Then he said, "What do you have in your house?" "All I have is some oil," she replied. *As if that would do any good about now,* she thought. Her thoughts were interrupted by his strange instructions. "Go and borrow empty vessels from all your neighbors. When you have gathered them all, shut the door behind you and your sons, pour the oil into the vessels, and set aside the full ones. *What?...All right, it's not as if I have anything to lose. I don't understand how this is supposed to work, but then again God moves in mysterious ways,* she mused as she went off in search of her neighbors' vessels.

As she looked at the pitiful supply of oil and all the pots scattered around her, she shook her head and looked toward heaven. Okay, here goes...she turned the urn toward the mouth of the first empty vessel and began to pour. As the oil filled it, she gazed in wonderment. There had not been that much oil in the first place! She turned to pour what was left into the next container, and the next and the next, until she was out of containers. She couldn't believe it! But then again she could. Elisha had made the supernatural so real to them.

Elisha! She should let him know what had taken place! Upon her arrival, he gave her further instructions, "Go and sell the oil. Pay your debts and you and your sons live off the rest." Humbled by the faithfulness of God and these simple instructions, she went off to do his bidding.

SHE COULD HAVE: Grown bitter and turned her back on God. Been too prideful to state her need and too distrustful of Elisha to follow his instructions. She could have become paralyzed by resignation and a lack of faith.

WHAT SEPARATES THE DIVAS FROM THE GIRLS: The refusal to settle for less than what God has promised operating fully in their lives. The courage to be transparent in stating their needs and the humility to follow instruction without questioning, knowing that God will show up even if they don't know how.

LIFE LESSON: It ain't over 'til it's over, and with God, it never is.

> *Be anxious for nothing, but in everything by*
> *prayer and supplication, with thanksgiving, let*
> *your requests be made known to God* (Philip-
> pians 4:6).

A Diva Knows How to Work It

Don't believe the hype of the "name it, claim it, and frame it" crew. You've got work to do. Faith without works is dead, as James tells it in the first chapter of his letter to the church. True divas know they must work their faith, partnering with God to bring about some of the things they desire in life. Miracles are God's extras, wrapped in pleasant surprises of grace. The day-to-day grunt work is done by those who have been empowered by God to carry out His work here on earth and glorify Him in the process. He uses every trial, every area of lack, every mistake if we let Him, to further display His ability to overcome all we may suffer through. The key word here being *through*. Remember with God, it is all about the process of becoming. The only way that happens is if we go through some things. If He yanked us *out* of them early, our growth would be stunted, and we would not become more like Him. We would remain as we are, and for many, that is not a pretty picture. We would also be a grave disappointment to God, who had greater things in mind for us all.

What is our part in the drama of trials and life's inconvenient moments, when things are not exactly the way we would like them to be, or worse yet, difficult, uncomfortable, and downright *all* wrong? Our diva widow made all the right moves even when she couldn't fathom the outcome, and she learned some valuable lessons along the way that she can now teach us.

1. Know your rights.
You must place a demand on the promises of God, but not in the sense of being disrespectful. And certainly God does not need to be reminded of His promises to us. We need to build up our own spirits by rehearsing who He is and what He has promised so we can take the faith walk we need to claim what we want from Him.

Here is where what you don't know will hurt you. You must know the Word of God, His promises, and what your relationship with Him entitles you to. This widow who went to Elisha knew God had to do something based on her and her husband's relationship with Him. Her husband had served Him wholeheartedly, and she knew God would honor that because He said He would. If you don't know what God has promised you, you will never have the good sense to ask for it or claim it. This widow knew she was in right standing with God, and God had promised to provide for her. That little bit of information was enough for her to go on, the rest of the details she would get from the man of God, the prophet who knew how to tap into the promises and power of God.

When you know the God you serve—what His heart is like and what His promises are concerning you when life threatens to do you in—you can boldly refuse to "go out like that" as we say in the 'hood. Stand your ground and know what you can rightfully expect from God. Don't waver or compromise your prayers or faith.

This can be confusing for some. When do we get specific in prayer, and when do we just throw up our hands and say, "Let Your will be done"? Those of the fatalistic persuasion prefer the latter because then they never have to think or do anything. Then they grow despondent when they feel God has not responded to their willingness to be turned whichever way the tide pulled them. But the truth of the matter is, How do you know He answered if you never asked for anything specific? Dare to say what you want, understanding that God always answers prayer even if the answer is "No." Let me clarify. Being open to His will does not make you a victim or a mindless pushover, it merely means you are open to better suggestions and willing to act upon what He says versus what you think.

God invites you to have an opinion and an idea about how things should go in your life because He made you in His creative image. Every now and then He might allow us to wander into a situation where we can't find the answers. Maybe He does this just to get our eyes back on Him in a more focused way that takes us to a whole new level of submitting to Him. In this place, He meets us and reminds us of His graciousness to always see us through and to build our faith to even greater heights of absolute trust in Him. Therefore, have a position when you approach Him— one of trust in His Word and what He has promised you. If you know nothing else, know that He has asked you to cast your cares on Him because He loves you and He promises to faithfully supply *all* of your needs according to *His* riches, not your personal reservoir (Philippians 4:19). 'Nuff said. That takes most of the work off of you already.

2. State your case.

Jesus died so that you could have the right to do just that. The veil was rent and access was granted to boldly walk into the throne room and make your requests known to God. Not stating your need is not exhibiting your faith, it is uncovering your pride. How many times does God say to come to Him and tell Him what you want, tell Him what you need? He has the shoulders to carry the mother lode, you do not. Life is simpler than we think. We just get fooled by the weight of it when we try to carry it by ourselves.

Be specific. What exactly is going on with you? Now is not the time to go into denial. It is time to get real because you need answers, and you need them now. To continuously wonder what to do in the midst of your situation is a setup for falling into sin. At some point, you will get desperate and resort to the wrong measures to solve your problem. So say it like it is. If you need to seek counsel, go for it. This is about doing what you have to do to get back on track with victorious living. That will not happen if you are in an unresolved state or area of lack. Don't whine. Just be clear on exactly what you are dealing with and what your needs are in order to overcome.

There is a fine line that must be drawn in our attitude toward God when we are going through difficulties. The attitude should never be that He owes us—because He doesn't owe us anything. He has already given us everything. In that light, our attitude should be that we are coming to Him because He promised us something and we believe Him. He is able and willing to fulfill every promise, and it pleases Him when we remember what He says. In an attitude of trust, we can go to Him knowing what He has said about helping us in our situation and ask Him to do just that.

3. Follow instructions.

Yes, there will be instructions. For every question you ask God, He will either ask you a question or give you an instruction. Do what He says. We must get over the myth that God is sitting in heaven waving magic wands over people's lives. For the most part, He is active as a counselor who instructs and empowers His children to do His will. After we have done all we have been instructed to do, He takes over and does what we cannot do. Understand and know you will have a part to play in the story. Faith without any action is dead.

Perhaps the reason we wait until the last minute to pray is because we don't always want to hear what God has to say. Some of the dramas of life are of our own making, others are not. In either case, God has a word of instruction. It might be something as embarrassing as "So stop spending then," to something as profound as "Stand still and see My salvation, I've got this one." Whatever His instruction is, do like they say on product disclaimers: *Follow the directions to avoid irritation or injury.* Yes, you willful thing you, God's instructions really are for our own good. When we follow them, it leads to righteousness, peace, and joy in the Holy Ghost. When we don't, it leads to gloom, despair, and agony. It's a simple choice.

God's instructions might direct you to include others in the solution. Dealing with the humility of soliciting help is enough to send some people over the edge of avoidance and into a permanent place of being stuck. Yet God created us to be beings that depended first on Him, and then on one another. Independence just doesn't work well in a body where all the pieces need to work together. What others sometimes do not have in resources, they make up for in ideas, instructions, and useful connections. So ask and you will receive either the thing you've asked for or the instructions on how to get it. It's up to you to do the leg-work.

4. Use what you have. Pour it out and increase.
Something about being full of ourselves just doesn't work when we need something from God. Becoming empty vessels, open and available for whatever He wants to pour into our spirits, our minds, our hearts, and our character, places us ahead of those waiting in line for their problems to be solved.

The widow was instructed to collect empty vessels from her neighbors and then to pour what little oil she had left into them. Sometimes what we need is already in our midst being sadly overlooked. Sometimes what we have needs to be joined to what someone else has in order for the increase to begin. The bottom line is that something had to be poured out in order to become more. We could get really spiritual here, and look at this deeper, by concluding that until you get you out of the way by pouring out all that you are and have before God, there will be no room for more.

What exactly does that mean? At any given point along the journey of life, you can get saturated—so full of all you've been experiencing there is no room left for something new. You sense a discontent rising within, but you can't quite put your finger on what is out of place. The problem is not what is out of place, but where you are in the big picture of God's plan for your life. You should always be growing. But with any productive vine, there comes a time when the branches must be cut back to make room for sweeter fruit. Yes, there is already fruit on the vine, and you could be very happy with that, but the goal should always be sweeter, richer fruit coming forth in your life. Something needs to be poured out or trimmed back. Not necessarily gotten rid of, but dispensed to the right place.

The glorious thing about emptying yourself out to God or others is what you find out in the pouring. There is more where that came from. More love, more provision, more grace, more everything! The more room you make for God to move in your life, the more He will. You will only get as much as you make room for. When the widow ran out of pots, the oil stopped flowing. We need vessels to pour into: friends, strangers, family, others, to keep the flow of God's spirit alive and creative within us. So keep reaching out. Keep pouring out. It is in the pouring that the answers for our own lives become apparent. The problems we thought we had become minimal in the scheme of the big picture. Or miracle of miracles, as we pour out to others, the answers we were seeking come from those we meet along the way.

Working with what we have gives us the momentum we need in order to propel ourselves to the place of victory and the meeting of every need. What we perceive as nothing could actually be something of great importance—the key to getting what we need. Take hold of it and pour.

5. Put things in order.

For every lesson not learned, we are destined to repeat it. When we finally get the answer to our prayer, we need to take the steps to solidify the victory. In most cases, when God answers us, He doesn't just give us what we asked for—He blesses us beyond measure. Now is the time to practice good stewardship of what we have been given.

Our first reaction when emerging from a trial or receiving the answer to a long-awaited prayer is to heave a big sigh of relief and move on to the next project. But Elisha gave the widow specific instructions once all the vessels were filled with oil: "Go and pay off your debts and then live off the rest." God will always give you an overflow designed to address your current need and offer provision beyond the moment of your trial. Be a wise steward. Do not frustrate the grace of God by taking for granted what He has given. The enemy of our souls always stands ready to steal, kill, and destroy. With a grateful heart, cherish what you have been given and use it wisely. Whether it is money, or love, or even health, never take it for granted or assume it will always be there. Do the work it takes to maintain the level of living, loving, and overcoming that God has designed for you. Pace yourself so you can finish the race. Endurance will get you through the marathon. And that is exactly what life is. With our faith focused on the finish line, we are called to keep our eye on the prize—the high calling of a life well-lived in honor of Christ Jesus. A life that blesses others and glorifies His Name. A life that tells the rest of the world, so badly in need of something to believe in, we can believe God's promises.

Diva Confession

I will neither question life nor resign myself to circumstances. By faith I will embrace the promises of God and utilize the strength and instruction He offers in order to overcome my trials.

Diva Reflections

✳ How do you respond in the face of lack, disappointment, and trial?

✳ Who do you blame when you are going "through"?

✳ How is your prayer life at this time?

✳ Are you open to instruction?

✳ How long does it take you to exhaust your own solutions before coming back to God?

✳ What perspective do you need to gain on your circumstance?

✳ Who else could be of help at this time?

✳ What things do you need to empty yourself of right now?

✳ What could you pour out in order to be a blessing to someone else?

✳ What steps do you need to take so you never revisit this issue again?

The Divine Bottom Line

Until we surrender what we want, we walk with clenched, empty hands. In God's economy, only what we pour out by faith can be increased in our lives to overflowing that not only fills us, but blesses others.

Leave a Lasting Impression

Like watermarks
etched in onion paper,
clearly seen in the light,
her life left its mark
on countless lives.
Like faint whispers,
the sound of her laughter echoed in their spirits...
Her soothing touch was felt in the wind
reminding them of her
and the remnants of her sage advice that
hung like velvet curtains in their minds
every time they were tempted
by the foolishness she warned them against.
And in the still of the night,
they could see her in their dreams,
weaving her acts of kindness
like rich tapestry
in their lives that told a story
of how she had loved them,
touched them,
blessed them,
freed them to love like she did.
A soundless example
again and again
in tribute to her
throughout the ages,
the finest compliment that could be rendered
was that of imitating a life
well-lived.

THE DIVA LEGACY

*M*ore often than not, it's not the immediate moment that will tell your best life story, it will be the memories you leave behind. We are called to live lives that contribute to the big picture of the world and God's kingdom. If you miss that one vital truth, then truly your life will never hit the threshold of fulfillment you were created to experience. You are to be fruitful—bearing fruit that is not just a temporary filler, but rich fruit that will remain. The substance, as well as the fragrance of it, should bring pleasure to God and nourishment to the soul of everyone you encounter.

What will be said about you after you have transitioned on to glory? Recently I went to a funeral that was a celebration. Countless people paid tribute to this woman who had brought so much love and laughter to each of the lives present. It was hard to be sad because there were just too many wonderful memories. There were so many things that made us chuckle and laugh out loud as we remembered one deed after another, always accompanied by a hilarious remark, a signature of her incredible sense of humor. We all decided our lives were the richer for knowing her. She left fruit that remained in the form of sage advice, the listening ear she had, meals prepared, and things made for people. Special memories of her kindness and concern, her genuine interest in each person who knew her, the smallest detail she would remember made us feel all the more significant. She was a diva—a woman who possessed the divine attributes God wants every woman to have.

The divine bottom line in life is we all want to make a mark, to leave something that counts behind, to truly matter. It is the deposit we make of Christ Himself in the lives of others, giving selflessly and joyfully. His love compelled Him to give everything. And even though everyone did not receive Him, He gave anyway. Love does not count the cost or keep a record of returns. Love just loves, and for this reason alone, it is the most desired of all things on earth. A diva who masters the art of loving will lack for nothing, and everyone she encounters will be the richer for knowing her.

Divine Contribution

 each woman is born a gift to the world. Simply by being who she is, following the inclinations of her heart, she will make and leave her mark. How will this be achieved? By following and obeying the law of love that Christ puts in her heart. Unconditional love will always choose the higher good in every situation. It seeks to touch lives and leave a deposit that will heal, transform, and bless. When we gaze at our limited resources and overlook the priceless gifts within, we are tempted to believe we have little to offer. Nothing could be further from the truth. For every offering, no matter how small, is significant if given from the heart. It is the heart-to-heart connection that remains and sustains a lasting legacy. It is in that legacy that we are given the ability to remain alive forever. One diva discovered the power of this truth in a most miraculous way. (Read Acts 9:36-43.)

Behind the Veil

The mourners gathered, clinging to different pieces of garments and trinkets. Cradling them as if they were sacred, they recalled the dead woman's many kindnesses and charitable deeds, citing what a reflection of God's love she had been. How Tabitha, or Dorcas as some called her, would be missed! She had been a faithful disciple of the Lord and practiced good works. Not a sweeter woman could be found in Joppa. If she was not encouraging, she was advising. If she wasn't advising, she was simply listening, making people feel as if she had heard and felt every word. Her door, as well as her heart, was always open. She had nurtured widows in their bereavement, extending not just hospitality to them, but tirelessly giving provisions such as sewing beautiful tunics and garments that she bestowed upon them with the humility of a servant. The recipients of her love and generosity had been by her side as she convalesced, struggling against the illness that claimed her. Now their grief was inconsolable, for losing Tabitha was like losing a part of themselves, so intricately had she been woven into the fabric of their lives.

After washing her and gathering to memorialize her, they heard Peter was in nearby Lydda. They could certainly use his teaching and words of encouragement now. Sending for him and pleading with him not to delay, they hoped against hope he would include them in a schedule they knew was filled with tireless ministry to many. Blessing of blessings, he arrived filled with sympathy as they poured out their grief and their tears. But they found his reaction rather strange. He accompanied them all to the door, and then shut it behind him, separating them from their beloved friend. What could he be doing? Perhaps his grief was so strong, he needed to weep alone. And so they waited...

Finally, the door opened and Peter beckoned them inside. There sat Tabitha alive and well, praising God as she always did. Their joy could not be contained as they spilled into the streets after embracing her and celebrating with her.

They had to spread the word. Not only was Jesus alive and well, so was Tabitha as proof of His power to heal, save, and deliver! What more proof did anyone need in order to claim such a rich salvation? Truly her deeds in life had given small revivals to many a heart, but her miraculous recovery from death brought revival to their world, their community, beginning a ripple effect that spread throughout the region. Once again Tabitha was doing what she did best—touching lives and transforming them eternally.

SHE COULD HAVE: Lived a self-centered life enjoying what she had as a woman of means without a thought to those less fortunate than herself. She could have had a more surface approach to charity work, treating others as projects and not really getting involved in their lives because her contributions were enough.

WHAT SEPARATES THE DIVAS FROM THE GIRLS: Hearts that follow their work by becoming personally involved in touching those with needs. The ability to have such a lasting effect in the lives and hearts of others, leaving fruit that remains in every life they touch.

LIFE LESSON: The life we create now is the life that remains after we are gone. Acts of selfless love serve as worship to Him who created us. These acts give others the precious gift of knowing and believing they are precious in the eyes of God and that they matter to humanity. This is the source of life and evidence of a life well-lived.

> *Whoever seeks to save his life will lose it, and whoever loses his life will preserve it* (Luke 17:33).

Divas Live Forever

In the search for significance, the motivating factor must be contribution empowered by love. Then, and only then, will people see and experience our authenticity, which leads them to respond to us in ways that warm our hearts and lets us know we've made a lasting difference. In the end, it's not about us. We were created to serve, to give, to die to ourselves over and over again, as many times as it takes for others to be healed and empowered to live the life they were created to live—one of hope and joy. We are the arms of God and His representatives in the earth realm. We are the conduits of His goodness. The more we pour out, the more we receive.

In giving, the cycle of life, love, and well-being is regenerated again and again. The true miracle of living and loving according to God's design is manifested in its fullness as everyone gets blessed in the exchange. Tabitha lived a simple life, but one significant enough to get the attention of a community and a God determined to bring her back to life. She was brought back from death, bringing revival for those around her. We are all given this opportunity to arise from a life of death, bound by our own selfish pursuits, to truly live by giving. Tabitha's life gives us some parting principles to keep us reminded of what is truly important.

1. Be faithful.

Live life 100 percent in all you do. Be sold out, totally committed to everything God has placed in your world. So many merely skim the

surface. They glaze over their faith, their mar-
riages, their work, their life. A life lived with
complete commitment to all you are afforded
is the richest life of all. It doesn't matter how
much you have or don't have in this scenario,
it is the quality of life that makes all the difference in the world to you and to others.

Living a life filled with passion for what you believe, for
your work and purpose, for your relationships, for others in
need will be your catalyst in being faithful to what you were
created to do. Nothing is insignificant when you are passionate about it. Commitment is the cornerstone of a life
that is lived with integrity. Integrity will still be telling your
story long after you are gone.

What do you give yourself to? Are you all in or simply
going through the motions? Being completely present and
patient is also part of being faithful. Everything within you
must be focused on the moment, on the person, on your
God in order to effect any contribution that will make a significant difference. Be willing to wait on the outcome. Be
faithful even when it looks as if nothing is happening. Just
keep doing what you do. This is true discipleship—to
follow the divine leader without questioning, walking in
trust that the answers will be made clear along the way.

Keep the faith even when others don't seem to appreciate your contributions. Remember, every flower doesn't
sprout exactly where the seed was planted. Roots travel.
They travel to where the ground is most fertile and accom-
modating.

Be faithful even when you can't see God moving

because He is still at work. It is in the time when you see Him moving the least that He is up to the most. A diva never abdicates her position of faith because it is based on the knowledge that no matter where she finds herself, she is still blessed above measure...and the best is yet to come.

2. Be fruitful.

Don't be afraid to give the flowers you have away and make room to cultivate more. We were created to bear fruit that doesn't disappear after one sitting. It should remain in fragrance and in sweet aftertaste. It should take root in the person who partook of it and sprout again to become an offering to someone else. True fruitfulness is more about what you plant than what you harvest for yourself. Harvest is an automatic given. What you sow you will reap, so plant well and be fruitful.

What exactly does this mean in layman's terms? Let's start with your thoughts. What you think about yourself, others, and God will affect what you do. What you do will garner one type of reaction or response, which will then solidify your views on how you will approach life. If you believe there is no profit in giving, when you give something to someone and they don't respond the way you wanted them to, it will be confirmed in your heart you were right even though you were actually wrong. However, if you believe you were created to give and that giving pleases God, a person's response to you will have no effect on your future actions. Decide your attitudes *before* life shapes them for you.

Now let's think about what you say. Words have power. They set things in motion in your heart, your mind, and in others. Words move people, spiritual principalities, and God. What you say will manifest in the responses of others, as well as affect your life. What you expect is what you will speak, and what you speak is what you will get. In many instances, we speak before we think and then wish we could snatch back what was said, but the damage has already been done. To think before speaking is an amazing gift. It affords you the power to create a world for yourself that works *with* you instead of *against* you.

This is wisdom at work, and wisdom is always fruitful, setting her banquet table with fare that is rich and filling for those she serves. Allow the law of kindness and sound instruction to be on your tongue, planting seeds of soundness in others that motivate them to make the right choices in life. Then watch the harvest that comes from words well placed, planted deep in the spirit and bearing rich fruit that feeds not just your soul, but also countless others.

Last but not least, think about your works. What you do will last forever. Plant carefully. How many people have we seen in the media who have been haunted by past mistakes at the height of their success? All that they worked for crumbles to ash before them because the world can be an unforgiving place. God is faithful to restore us in these instances, but we can avoid many heartaches by making sound choices.

What you plant with your hands will bear a harvest. In Tabitha's case, she planted thoughtfully because her actions gave evidence of her inner attitude. She planted words of encouragement and faithful instruction. And she also planted with the work of her hands by sewing garments for the needy and widows. All she had she gave, harvesting a rich and bountiful crop of love, appreciation, and honor.

3. Give of yourself.
It is not what you give materially that makes the difference, it is the spirit in which you give. It is easy to give things and divorce yourself from the exchange. True giving comes from the heart. It requires you to give of yourself.

The difference Tabitha was able to make was not because of the garments these women received, it was her, the whole person. They knew each thing they received from her was a labor of love. It was an investment of herself that came from a heart that embraced them in their suffering and need. They knew they were not just another charitable project. They were vitally important and significant in Tabitha's mind, and that made them feel important, affirming that their lives mattered and they had something to contribute not based on the measure of external goods. Because she gave of herself, they learned to give of themselves to one another. With her departure, they did not fall apart; rather, they came together in honor to her and in support of one another.

The beautiful thing about people who give from the heart is their spirit becomes contagious to others. The effect is far reaching because people are moved to consider their own heart motivations and make changes in their lives.

Moving past the walls they've erected for their own safety by observing the life of one who gives selflessly, folks learn there is no danger in becoming vulnerable and sharing from a heart that actually feels those around them. They discover a new joy, a new sense of purpose that both fulfills and invigorates them to greater acts of service. This is the love of God reflected in all its fullness. God so loved the world that He gave; He gave of Himself by sacrificing His Son, the thing dearest to Him. He did not draw back because everyone did not appreciate or acknowledge Him. No. He remained His authentic self, giving everything anyway. In the end, He will gain everything. Divas know that the only way to have it all in life is to give it all away. Pouring out is not about coming up empty, it is all about making room for more—more love, more joy, more of all your heart's desires.

4. Be a source of revival.

Life. That is what we were created to give. "Be fruitful and multiply" was the first assignment given to the man and woman in the garden. It is the essence of kingdom living. The room should change when you walk in because you bring more life into the atmosphere. The life you carry within you by the spirit of the living God is the same life you dispense to others through thoughts, words, and deeds.

The words you speak can change people. The kindnesses you extend can transform hearts. With the impartation of life, you can start a bonfire that burns and lights the way for others. A heart revived from brokenness becomes a beacon of hope to someone else who is suffering. Your life should provoke and stir others to good works, to thirst and hunger after righteousness, to desire the experience of kingdom living. They will want to know God because you make it look so good. The world is waiting for examples that reflect who God truly is. Now is your chance to show them. It takes one match to light a fire. Partner with God and light it. Let the Holy Spirit blow on it, and watch it spread the contagious good news of what God has prepared for those who love Him. Let your life tell the story. Don't say what you can't live. Tabitha's life told the story. Her resurrection was the wind that blew on it. We, too, get the chance to be resurrected in the hearts of others long after we're gone based on what we deposit into their lives. Always give life.

A true diva leads by divine example, dispensing truth, light, and life to everyone she meets. The things she shares continue on as the one she touches or influences tells a friend or mimics her behavior, and that is passed on to another friend, and so on, and so on. The chain reaction begins...the kindling of revival. How great a fire a little spark can start! The spark may be as minute as a reassuring smile. A look that says it all. An act of graciousness or the extension of grace to someone who does or sometimes doesn't deserve it. Always be ready to address a need that might otherwise go overlooked.

Breathe life onto others' dreams. Pour life into thirsty spirits. Give life to weary arms with words of encouragement and insight. Continually give hope and sustenance. Revive and nourish wherever God leads you. Flourish in the midst of every opportunity to give of yourself. Let your example be the essence of life like a sweet perfume that lingers in the air long after you are gone.

Diva Confession

I will not overlook the opportunities afforded me to give life to those around me. I will plant seeds that will produce a legacy of life, hope, and joy in the lives of others, trusting God to give the increase in the appropriate season.

Diva Reflections

✳ What deposits are you actively making into the lives of those around you?

✳ What is your motivation for giving to others?

✳ What area of need are you drawn to in others?

✳ How can you give life to others in that area?

✳ Write down what you would want your epitaph to say.

✳ Does your life reflect what you have written?

✳ Make a list of the legacy you would like to leave behind in the lives of your family, your friends, your work associates, your community, the world.

✻ How will you work to make that a reality?

The Divine Bottom Line

The measure of life you give to others is the measure of life you will experience in your own personal kingdom. Grace for grace. We truly do get what we give.

From One Diva
to Another

*H*ow many stories I could tell of women who, against the odds, in spite of their mistakes, or what they viewed as their shortcomings or insufficiencies were qualified in God's eyes to become major divas. Their acts chronicled in the Bible serve as an example of what is possible in your own life.

Women like the mother of Moses, who understood her calling as a mother. She dared to save her son's life knowing he had been born on purpose with a purpose. She took her assignment to preserve his life and destiny seriously (Exodus 2). Or Elizabeth, the mother of John the Baptist, who found out it's never too late to give birth to the desires of your heart. If anyone understood the value of being sensitive to the Spirit of God, it was she (Luke 1). Or Rizpah, who understood a thing or two about preserving the honor of those who were unable to grasp it for themselves and convicted those around her to get their acts together without saying a word. Here was a mother who chose to watch over her murdered children, keeping their corpses from being devoured by scavengers until the king ordered their remains to be buried (2 Samuel 2:10). Or the

widow of Zarephath, who took a step of faith and wit-
nessed the miracle of increase. In spite of her own hunger,
she gave her last bit of bread to a prophet, trusting God
would supply for her (1 Kings 17:8-15). Or Eunice, who
chose to perform the ultimate act of being fruitful. She took
the time to teach and groom a young man by the name of
Timothy in the faith and watched him grow into a mighty
man of God (2 Timothy 1:1-5). So many women making up
a great hall of fame of those who personified the divine
attributes that lead to victorious living. It leaves no excuse
for us to walk in defeat. It leaves no excuse for not living
up to our full potential.

To be or not to be a diva? That should not be the question. Simply because you have no choice. You *are* a diva.
The question needs to be rephrased. What type of diva will
you be? One that reinforces the old stereotype of being
high-maintenance and self-centered? Or will you get over
yourself and be a gift to the world because you choose to
activate the parts of your God-given, God-centered nature
that mysteriously and wonderfully make you partakers of
His nature and participants in the divine? Hmm… That is up
to you, my friend.

To correspond with Michelle, log on to

www.michellehammond.com

For information on booking Michelle McKinney
Hammond for a speaking engagement, log on to

www.michellehammond.com

or call

866-391-0955

Other Books by
Michelle McKinney Hammond

101 Ways to Get and Keep His Attention
The DIVA Principle™
The DIVA Principle™—A Sistergirl's Guide
DIVA-tudes
Ending the Search for Mr. Right
Finding the Right Woman for You
Get Over It and On with It
How to Be Blessed and Highly Favored
If Men Are Like Buses, Then How Do I Catch One?
In Search of the Proverbs 31 Man
The Power of Being a Woman
Prayer Guide for the Brokenhearted
Release the Pain, Embrace the Joy
A Sassy Girl's Guide to Loving God
Sassy, Single, and Satisfied
Secrets of an Irresistible Woman
The Unspoken Rules of Love
What Becomes of the Brokenhearted
What to Do Until Love Finds You
Where Are You, God?
Why Do I Say "Yes" When I Need to Say "No"?